Teenage Stress

Selected books for young readers by Daniel Cohen

Southern Fried Rat and Other Gruesome Tales
The Last Hundred Years: Household Technology
The Last Hundred Years: Medicine
The Headless Roommate and Other Tales of Terror
Great Mistakes
What's Happening to Our Weather?
Creativity: What Is It?
Gold: The Fascinating Story of the Noble Metal Through
the Ages
The New Believers: Young Religion in America
Intelligence: What Is It?

Teenage Stress

by
Susan and Daniel Cohen

M. Evans and Company, Inc.
New York

Library of Congress Cataloging in Publication Data

Cohen, Susan.
  Teenage stress.

  Bibliography: p.
  Includes index.
  Summary: Discusses stress and its causes, what it
does to and for one, and how to keep the stress in one's
life at a tolerable level.
    1. Stress (Psychology)—Juvenile literature.
  2. Adolescent psychology—Juvenile literature.
  3. Adolescent psychopathology—Juvenile literature.
  [1. Stress (Psychology)   2. Stress (Physiology)]
  I. Cohen, Daniel.   II. Title.
  BF724.3.S86C63   1984   158'.1   83-16477

  ISBN 0-87131-423-1

M. Evans and Company, Inc.
216 East 49 Street
New York, New York 10017

Design by Nancy Kirsh Sugihara

Manufactured in the United States of America

9 8 7 6 5 4 3

Contents

1

You're Just Like Everybody Else

AS IT SAYS IN BILLY JOEL'S SONG "PRESSURE," LIKE EVERY-
body else you'll have to learn to face pressure, or to be
more precise, stress. Actually, you face it all the time. You
may not be able to define the word exactly, but most of the
time you know what it is when you feel it. You will recognize yourself and people you know in some of the following situations.

You're being torn apart, pulled in two different direc-
tions. Your parents are getting a divorce. Right now
they're having a big fight over the telephone. It's not much
different from the way they used to fight when they were
together. Only now, all you can hear is your mother shouting. No doubt at the other end of the wire your father is
shouting, too.

You head straight for your room, your sanctuary. Slamming the door is like putting up a big sign saying, "Keep Away," "Enter at Your Own Risk," "Off Limits," "Private Property," "No Trespassing," or just plain "Mine."

You throw your books on the floor. You have tons of homework to do tonight. You turn on the stereo loud and light a cigarette. You know your mother is so absorbed in fighting with your father she won't come in and start bugging you about what you're doing to your lungs, the way she usually does.

"Haven't I told you not to smoke? It's no good for you. It causes cancer."

"Well, *you* smoke."

"Yes, and look at what I go through every time I try to stop. When you get to be my age . . ."

"Aw, come on, cut out the 'my age' bit."

"Kids, they think they know everything. You'll learn, you'll see."

You blot out the rest of the lecture. You know it by heart—and you keep on smoking. It makes you feel better, and right now you need to feel better. You have a lot of big decisions to make. There are going to be a lot of changes in your life. You get a headache just thinking about the future. You don't have the energy to make any decisions. Your parents talk about going through a divorce as though it affected only the two of them. Well, aren't you going through it, too?

You're tense all the time now, you feel it especially in your stomach. You blow up at your friends about practically nothing. They're trying to understand—several have been through divorces, too, though not all of them. Why couldn't you be one of the lucky people who have parents who love each other and you?

Not that your parents aren't trying. Last weekend your

father tried to be extra nice. But it was all strained and phony. He wasn't there in the same way anymore. He had to check his engagement calendar to figure out when he'd see you again. You felt as if you were making an appointment the way you do with the dentist. When you got home you were depressed and tired.

Your mother couldn't hide her curiosity about the visit. She didn't exactly quiz you to find out what your father had said. Clearly, she had spent a lot of time with her therapist trying to figure out how *not* to react to the visit. But when she started telling you all the great things she'd buy you, you realized you were being bribed to prefer her over your father. You were so miserable by the time you got to bed that, tired as you were, you couldn't sleep. You've been having a lot of trouble sleeping recently.

Looking back over the last few months you wonder how you survived at all. Every time you walked into your house it was like walking into a battle zone. When your parents weren't actively fighting they kept away from each other in hostile silence.

The little daily things that needed to be done weren't getting done. Bills were piling up, supper wasn't ready. When you needed help for the math test you didn't get it. Talking to your parents was hard enough before. Now it was impossible. The chaos left you confused. You just couldn't think clearly anymore. Sometimes you went to school looking really lousy, and everyone noticed. You felt like an engine running out of control. There wasn't a single part of your life that didn't suffer because of what the divorce was doing to you.

Your friends tell you that when the divorce actually comes through, things will settle down, you'll get used to living in a new way. But you can't believe things will be better. Your body and mind have been so battered by a whole range of negative and painful emotions that you feel you will need a miracle to recover. Take stomachaches, for example; you never used to get them, but now you have them all the time.

And there are all the decisions to be made. Should you go live with your father or stay with your mother? Will you be able to go back to camp this summer? Your mother's already complaining that your father's skimping on the child support payments, and she's been telling you that things will be rough. There was never enough money before, so what are things going to be like now?

You hate your mother when she complains about your father. She's always probing his weaknesses. Yes, he can be brusque and distant. You know that better than anybody. But he isn't always like that. Your mother, too, has her lovable side, and that makes it harder. You can't just dislike your parents outright, and mixed feelings can be the most difficult ones to live with.

Maybe what you need is a dose of the grisly stuff they show on the six o'clock news, such as parents who beat you or something. At least then you'd have an excuse to turn on them both and do something drastic. You'd have a reason to hate them. Lately, you seem to have lost the will to do much of anything. You mostly sit here on the floor of your room, feeling dead.

Having the stereo on loud isn't helping this time. You know that your mother is still on the phone. You feel helpless. How can people say the teen years are the best of your life? If these are the best, what's to come?

You try to lose yourself in a daydream. You're smart, cool, terrific looking. All your problems are solved. You're making love to this absolutely sensational person. But you can't go away inside your head now. You've just got to get it together, got to study. Otherwise, you'll blow another test and that means another trip to the guidance counselor—your marks have gone all to hell lately.

But still you sit where you are, unable to move. If the roof caved in, you wouldn't have the energy to move. Does this inertia mean you're going crazy? It's one thing to feel weird and different—that's bad enough—but it happens all the time. The inertia is something else. One reason you notice every fresh zit that appears on your face is that you're afraid your appearance will give you away. You've heard emotional stress hurts the complexion. They'll know just by looking at you how insecure you are, how different. But being crazy is worse. It's terrifying. It means breaking down in front of your worst enemies or being locked up in a hospital. If you're going crazy maybe you'll kill yourself. There are times when dying seems like the only way out of the mess you're in anyway.

You hear footsteps. The phone call is over and your mother stands outside your room. You can hear her crying. That's all you need, your mother crying and telling you her troubles, expecting you to mother her. You need someone to tell your own troubles to. Who? Your parents are out. The guidance counselor's an idiot, and a therapist will find out you're crazy.

The numbness is growing worse, settling over you like a heavy weight. Your mother knocks on the door. You start thinking about running away.

Divorce, the death of a parent, a serious illness, the breakup of a long-term relationship, a move to a new city. All of these create major changes in your life, and all are major sources of stress. But it isn't just the big bad things in life that create stress. All of the unavoidable, everyday little hassles are also powerful sources of stress, particularly when there are a lot of them.

The radio comes on, and you wake up to this week's number one hit song. It's an average kind of day—nothing special to look forward to, nothing awful you want to avoid. Still, you don't exactly rush out of bed. You're tired, and it's nice lying here listening to the song.

By the time you get up you're running a little bit late, and your sister's taking a shower. Now there won't be enough hot water for you to take one, and you really needed a shower to wake you up. Feeling grouchy, you force yourself to get dressed. As you tie your sneaker your shoelace breaks. It's a small thing, but it sends you into a boiling rage. You lose more time looking for another shoelace, and then you can't find the right color. You change your shoes and go downstairs.

Your eggs are cold and your mother nags you about how slowly you move in the morning. Your father has drunk most of the coffee. Your kid brother tells you that your hair looks funny. You gulp down a little food and, grabbing a comb, head for the bathroom mirror. Your appearance depresses you. The clothes you thought would look good, don't. Your hair refuses to be combed. The shoes you're wearing make your feet look big. If only you looked like someone in a blue jeans commercial, cool and sexy.

But you don't, and your parents are practically pushing you out the door, so you take your notebook and run to the corner to catch the school bus. You miss it, and that means you have to walk to school.

Will your friends wait for you or will you have to enter school alone? That would be terrible. It's never a good idea to be alone in school, not even for a minute, or people get the idea you don't have any friends. On the other hand there are some outcasts whom nobody likes, and if you're seen with them it's worse than being alone. You become very tense when you notice one of them ahead of you, walking slowly, kind of hoping you'll fall in step.

You don't like to be mean to anyone, so you just walk slowly. Unfortunately, by the time you reach school the late bell has rung. Your homeroom teacher directs a few sarcastic remarks at you. Everybody else has a good laugh at your expense and you sit down, thoroughly miserable. You are beginning to get a headache.

In your first class you discover that you have forgotten your homework assignment. In math the teacher pulls a pop quiz and you're unprepared. At lunch you find out you're having a peanut butter sandwich and a Hawaiian Punch when the rest of your friends are having pizza. You try to clown around about it, but your jokes fall flat. So you're stuck eating your peanut butter and feeling weird and different.

You fall down in gym and get a big, ugly bruise on your face. It's embarrassing. You're sure everyone is staring at it as they pass you in the hall. By now you're so tense that when your best friend comes up to you at your locker you blow up over nothing. So now, as if things weren't bad enough, your best friend's mad at you.

The droning voice of your English teacher makes it easy for you to slip into a daydream. You have always been secretly in love with someone in this class. You often spend the entire English period awash in fantasies. Unfortunately, today the teacher calls on you, ripping you out of your daydream by telling you that if you don't pay attention in class you'll have to make up for it in detention. You feel stupid, you look stupid, and your self-esteem, which has been battered all day, gets another blow.

In study hall you watch your secret love hold hands with someone else. The book you needed for your social studies essay isn't in the library. The one extracurricular activity

you looked forward to all day, Key Club, is canceled because the club advisor is out sick. Now you won't be able to
sit around joking with your friends in Key Club.

You get on the school bus telling yourself you'll stop off
at the video games arcade in your neighborhood before
you go home, but when you reach into your pocket you
realize that you've lost the five dollars you had. When you
get home you find your kid brother and his friends have
taken full possession of the Atari, and you can't get near it.

Because of the fiasco with the peanut butter sandwich
you've been hungry all day. You open the fridge only to
discover there's nothing good to eat. And supper turns out
to be fish. It's your turn to carry out the garbage. The dog
has thrown up on your best sweater and the stereo's broken.

Your mother won't let you talk on the phone past seven
o'clock tonight because of the low mark you got on the
math quiz, so you do what feels like hours of homework.
At last, in desperation, you turn to the television and learn
that the horror movie you thought you'd see isn't showing
until tomorrow. You got the date wrong.

What a day! It's been nothing but a series of little hassles
and they've left you a total wreck. You feel exhausted but
too upset to sleep. Anxiety has left you with a stomachache
and an acute emotional numbness. It's been a crazy day,
completely crazy, and if it's like this tomorrow you'll shoot
yourself.

You climb into bed, pick up a book, and start to swear as
the light bulb burns out.

Another bad day, another day when you are subjected to a lot of
stress. But it isn't just the bad days, big or little, that are sources of
stress. Stress is created by the good things in life as well as the bad.

It's the best day of your life. Everything started out in the usual ordinary way, but when the mail carrier handed you the letter you got so nervous your hand started to shake. You'd been waiting for this day a long time, hoping against hope, telling yourself over and over that it wouldn't matter if you didn't get in. There are a lot of colleges. But down deep you knew it did matter.

When you realized that you'd been accepted to the absolute number-one college of your choice, you felt so excited you thought you'd explode. In a state of total euphoria you went screaming around the house, waving the letter. Your mother hugged you and rushed off to call all your relatives and tell them the good news. You wonder how you pulled it off, what with all the competition. They must have made a mistake, got your name mixed up with someone else. You start to giggle and you can't stop.

Of course they haven't made a mistake. You're in and you know it. You lose yourself in dreams of what the future will be like. You imagine yourself on the campus, think about the people you'll meet and the fun you'll have. One thing leads to another, and soon you're pretending to yourself that you're rich and famous. Well, why not? At the moment everything good seems at least possible.

You think back over how hard you've worked for this. You're not one of those people who just breezes through everything. You're a worrier. How many nights did you spend learning all that boring chemistry? How many hours did you give to preparing for the SATs? Well, it all seems worthwhile now. You'll be the envy of your friends.

It's time for lunch. But you're too restless to sit down and much too tense to eat. You feel confined in the kitchen. You've just got to get out and walk.

It's hard not to shout your good news to everyone on the street, but that would be ridiculous. Besides, you don't want people to think you're bragging. You know a lot of kids are going to be very disappointed when they get their letters, and a lot of parents are going to be disappointed in their kids.

Still, you can't quite wipe a little smile off your face. When you feel this terrific there's no way to hide it. Even the familiar sights around you seem brighter and more interesting than usual. You ought to do your homework, but you can't seem to concentrate on it or on anything else.

The bubbling happy feeling lasts all day. You try to come down from this natural high but you can't. That night you can't sleep. You feel awake and sexy. You want to go out and pick up someone good-looking, go out and get drunk, get laid. You touch yourself all over, play with your body, and lose yourself in wild fantasies until at last you fall into a fitful sleep.

When you wake up next morning you're still flying, but underneath you know you're really tired. You've got a little nibbling headache. When you do come down, you know that it's going to be with a crash.

You go downstairs for breakfast. Your mother takes one look at you and tells you how awful you look.

You reach for the cereal and you start to sneeze. Your face feels flushed, your feet feel cold.

Your mother looks surprised. "You're not getting a cold, are you? You seemed okay yesterday."

You dip your spoon into your cereal. The cereal tastes funny. You wonder how you could get sick at the happiest moment of your life. It seems a little crazy. But when you swallow, your throat hurts. Crazy or not, you're coming down with a bad cold. By noon you're barely able to talk.

Stress is created by the bad things in life that happen to you, and by the good things. Big important events in life put you under stress, but so do a lot of little things. Stress is everywhere. It is an unavoidable part of life. And stress isn't all bad. Sometimes it drives us to accomplish things that we might not otherwise even attempt. While excessive and harmful stress certainly has to be minimized, trying to avoid all stress can be equally harmful. It's like trying to avoid life itself.

It's time for school elections, and today you're going to the auditorium with the other candidates to make your campaign speech. You can't face it. A month ago the idea of running for class vice-president seemed a lot of fun. Now it doesn't.

A speech! You hadn't realized how scared you'd be, but the thought of sitting on stage staring out at a sea of faces next period makes your stomach do flip-flops. Oh, if only it were a month ago and you could have avoided this mess by not entering the election at all.

Your throat is dry and you drink a Coke eagerly, wishing you could hide in the cafeteria all day. You haven't felt this tense since you were in a piano recital three years ago. At least then all you had to worry about was making a mistake in front of a bunch of little kids and a lot of relatives. Now you've got to stand up and make an idiot out of yourself in front of everyone in your entire class.

Take your speech: It sounds so dumb, all the stuff about how you're a good student and will be a conscientious vice-president, and how you're qualified to win because you're in this and that activity. You just can't get up there and say such things about yourself. Panic sweeps over you; your hands begin to shake.

Since you have never felt worse, a desperate longing comes over you to feel better no matter what. It occurs to you that there is a way out—you can simply withdraw from the election. No one can force you to run or make a speech. What will your friends say? They've spent a lot of time making posters for you, getting your petitions signed, encouraging people to vote for you. They'll be ready to kill you if you're not on the stage making your speech next period. Next period? It's almost *this* period. The bell rings and you jump.

It's time. Your hands are shaking badly now. Everyone will notice when you give your speech. How humiliating! No, there is no way you can go through with this thing. Better to have your friends mad at you than to have the whole class decide you're a freak. It takes only a moment to go to the office and have your name withdrawn from the list of candidates. Nobody argues with you or tries to get you to change your mind. After all, this isn't the first time—people have withdrawn before. Still, you are totally numb when you walk out of the office.

The tension's gone and in its place is a terrible fatigue. You're so tired you could fall asleep in your locker if it were a little wider. You slip into the back of the auditorium so your friends won't see you.

Most of the people on the stage look as if they're waiting to be shot. What a relief not to be with them! The speeches start. Except for one or two class clowns, everybody's boring. It's a shock to realize that your speech, at the very least, would have been no worse. And you notice that other people have shaking hands and squeaky voices.

You also notice that they feel pretty good when they sit down, which is a lot more than you feel. The hard part's over for them, but it's just beginning for you. Wistfully, you remember why you wanted to run for vice-president in the first place. Now you've blown a chance to be on the student council, to have a special picture in the yearbook, and to make out with the superpopular kid who's running for class president.

If you had it to do over again, you wouldn't let the headache, fear, and tension stop you. But the speeches are over and all you can do is duck as your best friend and campaign manager heads your way.

We have looked at four very different situations, each of which produces stress. And there is a great deal more in life that produces stress. But what is stress?

Fifty years ago the word was hardly used at all except in fields such as engineering. Today the word is very fashionable in medicine, psychology, and everyday conversation. It is tossed about a good deal, and all too often it is used inaccurately. Stress is one of the most important medical and psychological concepts to be developed in the past half-century. In the next few chapters we are going to see how scientists discovered physiological and psychological stress. And we will find out more precisely what stress is and what it does to you and for you.

2
Stress-What Is It?

YOU'VE PROBABLY HEARD THAT WHEN PEOPLE ARE UNDER too much "stress" they can get sick or even die. Or that excessive "stress" causes "burnout"—that's another popular word today. You may have heard of dozens of techniques for "beating stress," and you may even have tried some of them.

The trouble is that most people who use the word *stress* either don't really know what it means, or they have the meaning all wrong. It is one of the most overused and misused words around. So we must start out by agreeing on what we are talking about. To do that we have to clear away a lot of false notions.

• Is stress the work pressure endured by people who are air traffic controllers, baseball team managers, or seventh-grade teachers?

• Is stress the demands placed on an exhausted mother by two cranky preschoolers?

• Is stress the emotional buffeting a child takes when torn between divorced and angry parents?

No. The situations that have been described may, and almost certainly do, create stress. But they are not stress itself.

• Is stress the butterflies you get in your stomach before a big test?

• Is it the midafternoon headache that sends a harassed mother reaching for the aspirin bottle?

• Is it the bleeding ulcer that fells the overworked executive?

No again. All of these symptoms, and many, many more, may be the result of stress, but they are not stress itself. Broadly defined, stress is what happens to the body when it is exposed to anything—nervous tension, disease, cold, heat, injury, and so on. It is the way the body in general responds to *any* demands made upon it. The word *any* is emphasized because as we have seen it isn't just the bad things that happen to you that create stress. Some of your happiest moments can also be your most stressful, and often stress can be created by conditions that you are not even aware of.

How the Body Responds

A lot of things happen to your body when you are under stress, but the body's reaction to stress is very complicated, and not all stress reactions are fully understood yet. Scientists have been able to measure changes that take place in certain glands, particularly the adrenal glands, the thymus, and pituitary gland, as well as in the lymphatic system. When a person experiences stress, these glands produce increased quantities of such powerful hormones as cortisone and adrenaline. The body's immune defense system, controlled primarily by the lymph glands, is activated. All in all, the body is preparing to defend itself and to resist change. Laboratory experiments have shown that long exposure to stress can produce permanent and damaging changes in the adrenal and other glands.

You can't feel your glands at work—not directly, anyway. However, as higher than normal levels of hormones such as adrenaline go coursing through your body, they produce some changes that you can feel. And these feelings are typical of a person under stress. See if you recognize them.

1. Your heart begins to beat rapidly. Sometimes it can be described as a "pounding of the heart."

2. You begin to perspire. Usually the perspiration appears on the palms of your hands. Your hands get clammy when you feel nervous. Other times it can be your armpits or forehead. Some individuals sweat profusely under even modest stress.

3. Your stomach seems to knot up.

4. Your mouth becomes dry and you may have difficulty swallowing.

5. You may get a tight feeling in your chest. When the stressful condition is relieved you feel as if you "got a load off your chest."

There are a few other reactions you can't feel, but which can easily be measured or seen by others.

1. Your blood pressure rises.
2. The pupils of your eyes dilate.
3. Your face may become flushed.

Stress can also produce some fairly obvious changes in behavior. One of them is what the scientists call *dysfunctional* behavior—you may drop or spill things, or suffer a temporary lapse of memory and become confused. Another common form of stress-induced behavior is called *overt* behavior—pacing the floor, waving your arms, biting your lip. These are some of the immediate obvious signs of stress. There is much more which is neither immediate nor obvious. But we'll get to that.

We said that stress—the same state—can be produced by any stimuli. Both good things and bad things—pleasure and pain, the physical and the emotional—all produce the same essential reactions in your body. This is simple enough to demonstrate. Take one of the most obvious and easy-to-measure signs of stress, your heartbeat as measured by your pulse. If you have been running or playing tennis, your heart beats faster and your pulse rate shoots up. Your pulse rate will also shoot up if you round a corner and are suddenly face to face with a large, angry dog. And if you round a corner and suddenly come face to face with your favorite movie star, your pulse will shoot up in just the same way it did when you saw a large, angry dog. Both fear and love make your heart beat faster. Both emotions are stressful, often as stressful as intense exercise.

It works the same way with behavior. If you have just received a piece of tremendously good *or* bad news, you are still likely to walk about, perhaps waving your arms and shouting.

How Stress Was Discovered

Traditionally doctors have looked at specific illnesses. A particular disease or other condition was caused by a particular virus or other factor, and it produced a particular set of symptoms. Psychologists took the same approach. A particular problem made a person feel depressed or nervous. But it was clear that all kinds of pressures, emotional as well as physical, could make a person feel tired and miserable and generally "run down" and "out of sorts." The symptoms were the same, no matter what the pressures. Doctors spoke vaguely of "weakness" and "nervous conditions," and might prescribe some sort of tonic or perhaps a good rest. And, of course, there would always be the advice, "don't worry, because worrying never solved anything." That advice is always easy to give but difficult to follow. Both physician and patient were aware that the diagnosis and prescription were inadequate. But given the state of medical knowledge at the time, there was nothing else that could be done.

Sometimes, and for some people, the pressures would simply become too great, and they would suffer from a "nervous breakdown." In World War I, soldiers who had spent long periods under fire in the trenches might be plunged into a condition that came to be called *shell shock*. Though they had not been physically injured, something serious had happened to them. No one was quite sure what had happened, but it was very clear that the shell shock victim could no longer function as a soldier. Symptoms could range from trembling and mental confusion to hysteria. In later wars the condition came to be called *battle fatigue,* but it was essentially the same thing. The exact cause could not be pinpointed, yet the condition was acknowledged as being as real as a bullet wound.

So in a very general and commonsense way, the effects of what we now call stress have always been recognized. But scientists cannot accept a principle just because it is something that "everyone knows." Too often what everyone knows turns out to be wrong. Scientists want to know exactly what happened, and if possible why it happened. The principle must be tested, not just accepted. Even today, the study of stress is still very much of a scientific and medical frontier; there are still controversies and vast stretches of unknown territory.

Some of the elements of modern stress theory can be found in the work of the nineteenth-century French physiologist Claude Bernard. He pointed out that all living beings try to maintain an internal balance, no matter what the changes in outside conditions. The most obvious example is that your own temperature remains constant no matter what the outside temperature, unless of course you are ill and have a fever or are exposed to real extremes of heat or cold. If the self-regulating power breaks down or is broken down by outside conditions, you are in serious trouble.

In the 1920s, Harvard physiologist Walter B. Cannon expanded on this idea with his theory of *homeostasis,* which means to maintain a stable state. Cannon discussed how the body must work to maintain inner stability, and when attacked must work to return to its previous condition of stability. The struggle for homeostasis can be a difficult one.

The lesson from both Bernard and Cannon was that the body engages in a constant and energy-consuming struggle against change. In a sense you can say that our bodies must run very hard just to stay in the same place.

Hans Selye and Stress

In the late 1920s, while Cannon was developing his theory of homeostasis, Hans Selye, who was to become the giant of stress research, was still a medical student in Vienna. As a medical student Selye saw patient after patient, but he was, as yet, too inexperienced to diagnose each patient's particular disease. Since he could not see the specific differences between the symptoms of different diseases, he was struck by the fact that most sick people were more alike than different. No matter what disease or injury patients suffered from—it could be a serious wound, a severe case of influenza, or cancer—most had certain characteristics in common. They lost their appetite, their strength, and their ambition or desire to accomplish anything. Usually the sick person also lost weight, "and even his facial expression betrays that he is ill," said Selye.

You can usually tell when someone is sick just by looking at him, even if you don't know a thing about medicine and haven't the faintest notion of what is wrong with him. Selye toyed with the idea of a syndrome, or collection of symptoms, of "just being sick." Of course, many other scientists had made similar observations but then forgotten them in the search for specific causes and symptoms of disease.

For nearly ten years this observation was relegated to the back of Selye's mind. But in 1936 the problem once again presented itself to him in a most dramatic fashion.

By this time he was working in a research laboratory at McGill University in Montreal, Canada. Like so many other European scientists, Selye had left Europe as the Nazis came into power.

Selye was conducting an experiment that involved injecting rats with different kinds of sex hormones. He found that it didn't make much difference which hormone he used, they all produced the same general set of reactions in the rats. At first he suspected that all the hormones were contaminated with the same type of toxin. But no, the hormones were pure. The different substances were producing the same reaction. In further experiments he discovered that these very same reactions might also be triggered by heat or cold, infection or loss of blood, and many other things.

When Selye dissected some of these rats, he could see clearly that changes had taken place. The adrenal glands had become enlarged and discolored. The thymus was shrunken. The stomach was often ulcerated. No matter what the rat had been exposed to, the bodily reaction was basically the same. The reaction didn't seem to be a specific response to the hormone, or the heat, or the infection—it was a general response to any or all of them.

When Selye first wrote up his discoveries for his scientific colleagues, he spoke of a syndrome produced by "noxious agents." Later he referred to the General Adaptation Syndrome (GAS). This was his term for the general bodily changes that take place as the body tries to adapt to some new set of conditions. Finally, Selye settled for the Biological Stress Syndrome, and it is under the title of *stress theory* that his work is now widely known.

Stress—A Confusing Word

When Selye chose a common word to describe his findings, he opened the door to a lot of linguistic confusion. Part of the confusion, Selye later admitted, came because "my English was not yet good enough." The word *stress* had occasionally been used, in a general sort of way, by doctors who might refer to the "stress and strain" of life. But Selye was more interested in using the word the way it was used in physics and engineering. To the engineer the word *stress* describes the forces that bring about changes in a structure, such as a bridge when any load passes over it, or in a piece of wire that is repeatedly bent back and forth.

Even today, when Selye's work is really quite well known, people still speak of cold stress or emotional stress. This is a confusion of the agent with the state it produces. Selye created the word *stressor* for the agent—cold is a stressor, emotions are stressors. The condition they produce is the stress. But the confusion persists, and it probably always will, at least outside of the scientific and medical world.

There are several other words that are often used, and misused, in any discussion of stress.

Tension. Properly speaking, tension refers to a contraction of the muscles. But one of the very common reactions to stress is a tightening of the muscles, so the two words are often used interchangeably. Since muscular tension is also often associated with certain states of mind—usually unhappy ones—we often speak of mental or emotional tension.

Anxiety. In its strictest definition anxiety is uneasiness of the mind. More broadly, it can be defined as imagined fear—a feeling of fear that exists where there is no clear or obvious immediate danger. Current brain research indicates that there is a subtle biochemical basis to much anxiety, and that some people are physiologically more prone to anxiety than others. All researchers agree that all of us can fall victim to anxiety, and that stress increases everyone's vulnerability to anxiety.

Emotion. This is a very general term. But a useful definition in this case is that emotion is the feelings you get in response to a given situation.

Selye's original experiments had been strictly with physical agents of stress such as hormones and temperature. He expanded his theory to include stress created by mental and emotional states as well. He wrote, "It may be said without hesitation that for men the most important stressors are emotional."

Fight or Run

That the emotions can cause physical reactions in the body was, of course, well known. Back in the 1920s Harvard's Walter B. Cannon first described what he labeled initially the "emergency" response. When we feel threatened, the body responds with all sorts of clear and measurable changes. A quantity of adrenaline is dumped into the bloodstream, the blood pressure rises, the pupils dilate, muscles tense, the heart beats more rapidly, and so forth. Many of these changes we would now identify as stress responses. What is happening is that very quickly, and entirely without conscious effort, the body is geared up to a high state of readiness. But readiness to do what?

Either to fight off the threat or to run away from it. The response is now commonly known as the "fight or flight reaction." We can't control this reaction any more than we can control the reaction of our bodies to produce antibodies that fight infection. Unfortunately, the fight or flight reaction is often activated at inappropriate times, and then it can hurt us.

It doesn't really make any difference if the threat is real, such as someone coming after you with a knife, or imagined, such as when you hear a noise and *think* someone is coming after you with a knife. The threat may not be physical at all, as when someone yells at you. Your body reacts the same way, though not necessarily to the same degree.

Whatever the degree, the fight or flight reaction can be exhausting. Once the threat has passed we may feel weak and tired. That's why people who have come through a crisis apparently without flinching will break down and cry once the danger has passed. Repeated activation of the fight or flight reaction can be very wearing on the body.

It is easy enough to understand how and why the fight or flight reaction developed. For people living in hunting and gathering societies, most threats are physical. Those who fight most fiercely and/or run away most quickly have the best chance of continued survival. This is the earliest form of human society, and throughout the history of human beings, people with poorly developed fight or flight reactions could nonchalantly make their way right into the jaws of a wild animal.

In the modern industrial world, however, the extreme fight or flight reaction is often, indeed usually, released in wholly inappropriate circumstances. While there are obvious physical dangers in our society, they are nowhere near as common as they were in the world in which the fight or flight reaction evolved.

Most modern "threats" are mental and emotional, not physical. If your teacher yells at you, your fight or flight reaction is stimulated. But you are not actually going to fight your teacher, though you might argue a bit. Nor are you going to run madly out of the room and down the hall. At most you might turn and walk away. So you don't really need the rush of adrenaline, the rapid heartbeat, and the rest of the physical preparation, but you get them anyway. That creates a wear and tear on the body—it creates unnecessary stress. In fact, your teacher doesn't even have to yell at you to trigger the response. It can be set off by just imagining what it would be like if your teacher yelled at you.

The ability to imagine what has not yet happened is one of the great glories of the human brain. It allows our species to look beyond the present moment, and this ability has doubtless contributed greatly to the success of the human race. But there has been a price attached. While we imagine what might happen, our bodies do not always make the distinction between reality and imagination. Just thinking about a problem creates physical reactions—creates stress. In the modern world it is the stress created by mental or emotional states that we have to deal with most often.

Walter Cannon was the pioneer in this area. He knew that in recognizing the fight or flight reaction, he had discovered something of importance, and he tried to encourage other doctors and researchers to take an interest in the subject. In 1927 Cannon told the Massachusetts Medical Society that doctors should have "a natural interest in the effects of emotional stress and the modes of relieving it. The field has not been well-cultivated. Much work still needs to be done in it. . . . There is no more fascinating realm of medicine in which to conduct investigations. I heartily commend it to you."

The Panic Attack

The fight or flight reaction is only one emotional remnant from a much earlier time. Another may be panic attacks. You've probably had them; almost everybody has. Suddenly, and for no very good reason, you get extremely nervous. You feel threatened. You begin to sweat and get butterflies in your stomach. You feel as if you want to scream and are about to lose control.

For some people panic attacks can come rather frequently, particularly when they have been going through an unusually stressful period. The attacks can be embarrassing and frightening, because it seems as if you're going crazy. You're not. Panic attacks are not a sign of mental illness. They appear to be some sort of evolutionary hangover. The origin of these attacks has been traced to activity in the brain stem, the most primitive part of the human brain.

If the fight or flight reaction helped prepare our ancestors for the dangers of life in the wild, what possible use could there ever have been for panic? One of the scientists who has studied panic, Dr. Donald S. Klein of Columbia Presbyterian Medical Center, has speculated that at one time sudden panic might have been an evolutionary advantage for small children. In traditional agricultural or hunting and gathering societies, if a child wanders away from his or her parents, the child is in great danger. If the child were to take the separation calmly and quietly, it might be a long time before adults or older children noticed the child was missing, and by then it might be too late. But if the separation quickly and automatically triggers panic, and the child begins to scream loudly, this attracts immediate attention and the child can be saved.

So panic is fine if you are a small child who has wandered away from your tribe while moving through the jungle. It's wholly inappropriate if you are a high-school student facing a tough test. Panic isn't going to help you pass. And worse still, you must expend a great deal of energy trying to hold down the feeling of panic. Just saying "don't panic" isn't much help if the reaction is automatic and uncontrollable. At least you don't have to feel that a panic reaction is a sign that you are going crazy or losing control. Some people just seem to have a biological vulnerability to panic. It is not a moral failing or weakness.

Panic tends to occur most frequently when we are already under a good deal of stress, and so our reserves of energy are low. It also tends to increase the stress, thus exhausting us further.

Three Stages of Stress

For most of his career, Hans Selye approached the study of stress from the point of view of a laboratory researcher trying to measure physical effects. In his work he found that the body had a three-stage reaction to stress. The first stage was what he called the alarm reaction—a usually brief but violent period during which the body's resistance to stress might actually go down. If the stress were great enough, a person or animal might not even survive this initial stage.

Usually this violent initial reaction subsides rather quickly, and the body enters stage two, resistance. During this stage the body has, to a degree, adapted to the stress. Bodily resistance rises to above normal levels and continues that way for quite a long time. But eventually, if the stress also continues at a high level, the body's ability to resist runs down. There can then be a quick sharp decline into the third stage—exhaustion—as resistance levels once again fall below normal. This time the direction can be irreversible; the subject can die.

These then are the basic principles of stress theory as developed by Hans Selye and others. It must be said here that not all scientists and medical professionals agree with all of Selye's ideas, some of which are still quite controversial. But these basic principles of stress theory have won wide acceptance in the scientific and medical community, and Selye's ideas have proved very popular among the general public.

The trouble with medicine is that it is not quite as neat and clear-cut as, say, mathematics. It is sometimes almost as much of an art as it is a science. You can make charts that illustrate how stress affects the body—in theory. In the real world, however, things are a lot more complicated. We have seen how all stimuli produce stress. But in addition to the general stress there are also specific effects. You fall and severely cut your arm. As a result you feel intense pain, and there is loss of blood and a number of other specific effects. You eat a tuna sandwich that has not been properly refrigerated and you get food poisoning. You get a bad stomachache and begin throwing up. These are also specific effects.

From the point of view of this book it is not these specific effects we are concerned with. We are interested in the general effects that are left once the specific effects are subtracted—that's the stress. The wound and the food poisoning produce very different specific effects, but they both produce the same stress. So does the flu, exposure to extreme cold, the breakup of a long-term relationship, or moving to a new school.

The effects of the stress hang on long after the specific effects have disappeared. Stress from a variety of different sources can build up in us. Often we can be under great stress and not even be aware of it. So we have to understand stress in order to understand why we often feel as we do.

Stress is responsible for or contributes to everything from sleeplessness and muscular tension to severe physical illness and depression. Too much stress can make us sick, but too little isn't good either.

While everyone undergoes stress, it does not affect everyone in the same way. A buildup of stress will attack the weakest link in our body's defenses. For some people even mild stress will bring on sleeplessness; for others it will be a headache, a stomachache, or a feeling of exhaustion and hopelessness.

Turtles and Racehorses

We can all tolerate different levels of stress. What may be a crushing level of stress for one person can easily be borne by another. Selye liked to speak of "turtles" and "racehorses." Turtles are people who can't take a lot of stress. They plod along. Racehorses are those individuals who not only tolerate a high level of stress but also sometimes seem to need it. Selye thought of himself as one of nature's racehorses, for he routinely worked ten or more hours a day for many, many years, under pressure. For people with his personality, it's inactivity that creates the most stress.

Hans Selye died in 1982 at the age of 75. He had had cancer for many years, but he continued his hard-driving, ten-hours-a-day work schedule practically until the end.

Selye suspected that his ability to cope effectively with the disease and the negative stress that it produced came from his unwillingness to give in to it. In a 1978 interview Selye said that this generally positive attitude "helped me a few years ago when my doctor told me I had cancer and had only a few months to live. I refused to retreat from life and was determined to keep working without worrying about my end. Perhaps this attitude helped my body combat the stress of my disease and subsequent operations, since as you see, I am still talking today."

We have spoken of stress being caused by poisons and viruses, by heat and cold, by injuries and emotion, by activity and inactivity. That is a fairly inclusive list. Is there anything that can happen to you that does not cause stress? No. Any weight on a bridge causes some stress in the metal. Any stimulus causes some stress in you. Stress is the result of the body's adaptation to change. Change is essential to life. The only time you will not be subjected to stress is when you are dead. So the problem of stress is not that stress exists, but the level of stress we must face, and our own individual reactions to it. Selye once said that a passionate kiss and sitting in the dentist's chair both create a good deal of stress.

Stress Is Not All Bad

In fact, we fall into a very serious trap if we regard stress only as a problem resulting from negative events—a disease, an accident, an emotional crisis. As we have mentioned, extreme stress can also result when good things happen, such as winning a big game, giving a star performance on stage, or falling in love. Any event that creates a tremendous emotional high is also creating a great deal of stress. Very often after such a high there is a period of letdown, fatigue, and depression. "I had such a great time last night. Why do I feel so awful today?" The feelings are very much the same as those you get after being faced with a very unpleasant experience, and they should be, for both are the result of the stress.

Selye and other scientists had a name for purely negative stress—*distress.* In everyday speech, stress and distress have become synonymous. The technical word for positive stress is *eustress,* though that word is practically never used in everyday speech.

At peak moments your muscles tense, your heart beats faster, increased levels of a variety of hormones are being pumped into your bloodstream. Once the peak moments have passed, the body must try to bring all of its biological elements back to their usual balance. It's the same thing that happens at moments of fear, anguish, anger, and other unpleasant sensations. It all causes wear and tear on the body. It all causes stress. For example, all of us sometimes crave the excitement that accompanies fear or tension. This is why people take part in dangerous sports, ride roller coasters, or go to horror movies. We deliberately place ourselves in very stressful situations, and we love it. Stress researchers speak of people becoming "drunk on their own hormones." For some this craving is harmless; for others it can lead to life-threatening situations.

There are plenty of cases on record of people who have gone to pieces after experiencing sudden success or good fortune. People were shocked when Freddie Prinze, a young comedian who had become a major television star almost overnight, shot himself for no apparent reason. In terms of stress theory such an "incomprehensible" action is not so difficult to understand. There was too much to adapt to. The stress was simply too great to bear.

Still, such cases are relatively rare. Everyone who has studied the subject of stress will admit that the stress resulting from good fortune seems much easier for most people to handle than the stress that results when bad things happen.

However, the idea that stress is not just negative or unpleasant, not just distress, must be kept in mind. That brings up another popular misconception, which is that stress is something to be avoided at all costs. This just isn't so. All stress not only shouldn't be avoided, it can't be avoided. As Selye said, the only time you are completely free from stress is when you are dead. Stress is the inevitable result of change and challenge, and change and challenge can be good for you.

Sometimes we think of highly stressful situations as being situations of great activity, but that isn't necessarily so either. Inactivity which results in boredom can produce a great deal of distress. So can social isolation. For many people just staying home and taking a rest is not always the best answer to stress-related problems. For some it may be the worst possible answer.

The purpose of this book is to help you understand stress, identify the sources of stress in your own life, and to give you some ways of dealing with it—so that all stress does not become distress.

3

Stress and You

FIFTY YEARS AGO THE IDEA OF BIOLOGICAL OR PHYSIOLOGI-
cal stress was barely recognized. Today it's a hot topic.
There are lots of popular books on stress, and magazines
and newspapers frequently carry articles on the subject.
From the television screen and on radio talk shows a variety of medical and psychological gurus offer advice on
how to "beat" stress. Stress has gone from obscurity to
become kind of a medical star—perhaps chief villain
would be a better description—for stress has been blamed
for practically everything. One thing is sure, stress is no
longer obscure.

Yet, as we pointed out, there are an awful lot of misconceptions about what stress is and isn't. One of the most
damaging misconceptions and one that this book has been
written to correct is this: Stress is not a major problem for

young people. Just look at what is currently being written and said about stress. A lot of it seems to imply either that young people don't exist, or that they exist only as a source of stress for older people but do not themselves suffer from stress-related problems. That, as you well know, is nonsense.

There has been a great deal of attention paid to certain types of stress-linked conditions, such as high blood pressure, heart disease, and ulcers, which are all primarily diseases of maturity and old age.

There has also been a great deal of talk about burnout—that's another trendy word used to describe a state of general physical and mental collapse brought about by prolonged exposure to excessive stress. The state has also been called hitting the wall. In the past, such a general collapse might have been called a nervous breakdown or nervous collapse. If you happened to be stuck in the trenches during World War I it was called shell shock; in later wars it was battle fatigue. It all means pretty much the same thing. But again, according to the media it seems to be only the adults, the business executives, soldiers, teachers, housewives, air traffic controllers and the like, who suffer from burnout because of the stresses created by their jobs and lives.

What about teenage stress or high-school student burnout? You know it's a real problem, yet it is one that far too many people are unable or refuse to recognize. Somehow the idea of stress and youth never seems to have become firmly associated. While lip service is often given to the problems of being young, adults all too often fail to take these problems really seriously. Whatever is bugging you can be brushed aside as a matter that is trivial, temporary, "childish," and generally something that is unworthy of serious, mature consideration and concern.

How often in your life have you heard statements like these:

"These are the happiest years of your life."

"Boy, do I envy you kids. You have no worries, no responsibilities."

"You've got your whole life in front of you. What are you complaining about?"

"You're young. You'll get over it."

"When you get to be my age you'll realize how unimportant all this is."

"When I was your age I never . . ."

Such statements can themselves add greatly to the stress you are already feeling, and they can send you into a towering rage, because they seem, and indeed are, so insensitive to the way that you feel.

Being young is supposed to be all fun and games. Stress is not supposed to set in until later in life, when you are faced with "adult" responsibilities. People who talk that way may have forgotten what it is like to be young. Perhaps in twenty years the problem you face right now will not seem so formidable. But you have to deal with it *now*.

Even those adults with faulty and selective memories should be able to learn something from the cold and frightening statistics on teenage suicide, alcoholism, and drug abuse. These are not statistics that come out of a stress-free time of life. They should make anyone recognize the awful toll that excessive stress can take on teenagers. It isn't just business executives and teachers who are suffering from burnout or who are hitting the wall. You can reach that state long before you reach your twentieth birthday.

The Most Stressful Years

Far from being a time that is free from stress, being young is probably the most stressful time of your life. Remember that stress is the body's response to any demands made upon it. There is no time in life when more demands are made upon your body than during your teens.

Change produces stress. Your teenage years are a time of unprecedented change. Not only are you changing physically, but your relationships with your parents, school, friends, and the world around you are also in a state of almost constant and radical change. It is a time when sex, one of the most powerful and stress-producing drives in life, comes into play.

These are just the natural and inevitable changes. Each individual also has a whole load of specific and stress-producing circumstances that he or she must adapt to. Usually, you have less control over the changes that are taking place in your life than an adult does. This powerlessness itself contributes to the stress. But you have more power and control over your life than you once did, not so very long ago. Your parents may resent or even fear this, and, in a hundred subtle, and sometimes not so subtle ways, indicate that they don't really trust you. That can be maddening and stressful.

And let's admit it, freedom, while desirable, is not always the most comfortable thing in the world. At one time in your life mom and dad made all the decisions. Now more and more of them are up to you. And you're responsible for the way things turn out. You wouldn't seriously want to go back to being a little kid again, when somebody else always told you what to do. But the new responsibilities take their toll. There are probably moments when you feel like sticking your thumb in your mouth and pulling the covers over your head. That's stress again.

We could go on, but you get the picture. No one really has to tell you that you are under a great deal of stress, because you already know that, even if others don't. Oh sure, in most cases you'll "grow out" of the problems that face you now, just as everyone keeps telling you. That's easy to say, once you are past them, but the problems are not at all easy to take when you are right in the middle of them. And people are often marked for life by their early experiences.

At moments it's tempting but not very smart to go to the other extreme, to panic over the stresses that you face now and inevitably will face in the future. It's just not useful to throw up your hands and say, "My God, how am I going to survive!" You'll survive, even if you feel at moments as if you won't or don't want to. Fortunately, nature seems to have provided a solution, or at least a partial solution, to the problem of excessive stress for teenagers—it is called adaptation energy, or it might simply be called vitality. You've got lots of it.

Adaptation Energy

Years of laboratory experiments convinced Hans Selye and other stress theorists that all living things, human as well as animal, possess a stock of energy that allows them to adapt to change. A fixed quantity of this energy appears to be something that all living things are born with. We draw on this store of energy throughout our lives, and when we use up our allotment the body can no longer adapt, can no longer withstand stress. The body falls into a state of exhaustion, and then we age and die. "The length of the human life span appears to be primarily determined by the amount of available adaptation energy," wrote Selye.

That, at least, is the theory. It was first developed over forty years ago, but the exact nature of this adaptation energy remains unknown even today. This is what Selye called "probably *the* most fundamental gap in our knowledge about stress." Stress theorists believe that once the nature of adaptation energy is understood, it can be used to fight disease and quite possibly to prolong life itself.

We do know that if the body is constantly exposed to any stressor, the energy will be used up. "That much is certain," Selye wrote. "We can verify it by experiment. We can observe that anything to which adaptation is possible eventually results in exhaustion, that is, the loss of power to resist. Just what is lost we do not know, but it could hardly be the calorie energy—which is usually considered to be the fuel of life—because exhaustion occurs even if ample food supplies are available."

There appear to be two types of adaptation energy, or at least two ways in which the energy is used. There is a superficial store of energy and a deeper reserve. Superficial adaptation energy can be restored by rest or change (we will get back to that shortly). It seems, however, that the superficial energy is restored primarily by drawing on the deeper reserves of energy which cannot be restored.

The biological wisdom of such an arrangement should be obvious. It keeps an individual from squandering vast quantities of this vital energy at any one moment. There are times when an accumulation of stress—good or bad— just wears us out. We become exhausted, perhaps even break down. We can't cope. We can't handle life anymore. We are forced to rest, to withdraw. But slowly, as the adaptation energy is restored, we recover, we can cope, we can handle things again.

However, it is the view of many stress theorists that the recovery of superficial energy does not mean total recovery of energy. It does not mean that nothing in the body has changed. Some of the deeper reserves have been drawn upon—they are being gradually depleted. But periodic depletion of our stores of superficial energy, which forces us to rest, slows down the drain on our deeper reserves.

People today are living much longer than they used to. For that reason more people ultimately succumb to the "wear and tear" diseases, the so-called diseases of civilization, or degenerative diseases, such as heart disease, cancer, and others, which stress theorists believe are diseases primarily brought about by stress.

When you are young your reserves of adaptation energy are at a high level. Not only do you have greater deep reserves of energy, you have the ability to draw upon them quickly, to make good the loss of superficial energy. You bounce back or recover from exhaustion far more effectively and completely than older people. In short, while both biology and society seem to confront the young with enormous stress, the young also possess the ability to take the stress and go on.

Restoring Your Energy

In order to handle stress effectively in our own lives, we must have a basic understanding of how it affects us. Laboratory experiments and general observation have shown that there are two types of exhaustion caused by stress, general and specific. General exhaustion is easy enough to recognize. Say you have been backpacking in the mountains, and at the end of the day you feel so tired that you are barely able to move, or even to think. That's only one form of exhaustion. Let's say that you have been doing difficult homework. After a few hours your mind may be tired, but you could still go out and run a mile, or play a game of tennis. Or if you have been worrying about something, then playing video games for an hour or so can be very "relaxing."

We put the word "relaxing" in quotation marks because neither running nor playing video games are activities that can properly be defined as relaxing. They require either a high degree of physical exertion or mental concentration—both stress producers. But they produce stress in a different area. Running after studying produces physical, not mental stress, thus it relieves the stress on an area that may already be nearing exhaustion. Of course, if you keep on running or playing video games you will reach a stage of general exhaustion.

A simple analogy is carrying a heavy suitcase. After carrying it in your right hand for a while that hand becomes very fatigued, so you switch to your left hand. When your left hand is tired you can switch back to your right again. Eventually, of course, you will become too tired to carry the suitcase with either hand. In the meantime you have been able to carry it a considerable distance, much farther than you would have been able to carry it if you had stuck doggedly to the one hand.

There is an old bit of medical folk wisdom that asserts "a change is as good as a rest." It appears that there is a great deal of truth in this old proverb.

The Stress of Boredom

Any sort of boring, repetitive activity can be extremely stressful. There is a famous scene in the Charlie Chaplin film *Modern Times,* in which Chaplin is working on an assembly line. All he has to do is tighten two bolts. It's a simple, mindless motion, but after his work is over he can't stop. He is still trying to tighten bolts in his sleep. In an exaggerated and comic way, Chaplin exhibits many signs of a person who has been subjected to extreme stress.

Anyone who has ever worked on an assembly line will testify that the work can be unbelievably fatiguing, even though it is usually physically quite easy. At one time the assembly line was thought of as one of the marvels of modern industrial society. It was supposed to "rationalize" the work process and make work more "efficient." It took quite a while for employers to realize that this "rational" and "efficient" process could produce terrible results. Workers quickly came to hate the repetitive tasks. They became fatigued, apathetic, and hostile. Often the quality of the work produced suffered badly.

But why should such simple tasks be so tiring? Objectively it would seem that just tightening a few bolts would not be very taxing mentally or physically. But that observation does not take stress into account, in particular the fact that in repetitive activities stress is concentrated in a small part of the body and mind. Experiments have shown that no one part of the body should be disproportionately overworked for a long period. When this happens, the body tries to protect itself from one-sided overexertion by spreading the feeling of fatigue throughout the entire body and through the mind as well.

In trying to analyze your own individual stress status, you have to consider not only the total amount of stress on your body, but also how it is distributed. If you are getting too much of one kind of stress, you need diversion, even if the diversion is another type of stressful activity.

The same is true for mental stress—indeed, diversion may be even more important in the area of mental stress. Let's take an example. Perhaps you have a chance to get a summer job in Washington working in a congressman's office. Since you have always been interested in politics, you really want this job. You also know there are other well-qualified applicants. Everything depends on an interview you are going to have with the congressman's assistant—tomorrow. Naturally you want the interview to go well, and naturally you are worried that it won't. There is nothing more you can do to prepare for the interview. All you do is worry about the things that can go wrong. The more you worry the more nervous you become, and the more nervous you become the more you worry about being nervous in the interview.

Everybody has told you to stop worrying. You have told yourself that. But it doesn't do any good. What you need is a diversion, some sort of general stress to take the place of the worry. Selye has said that by activating the whole body, the immediate source of worry becomes less important in proportion. Go out and take a long run.

The whole point of life cannot be to conserve one's

adaptation energy by avoiding all stress. That is not possible or wise, and the attempt will certainly lead to an extremely boring life. Some stress theory holds that each of us has a fixed biological level at which we are to expend our adaptation energy. If we exceed that level by being subjected to too much stress, that in turn leads to exhaustion, and ultimately to a harmful depletion of energy. But avoiding all forms of stress leads to boredom and a buildup of unspent energy—which can then turn inward in a harmful way. It is paradoxical but true that too little stress can itself be extremely stressful.

The problem of how much stress and what type is optimal is a very individual one. But the basic mechanism, the interplay between stress and adaptation energy, operates in all of us. As we understand this, we will be able to learn not only how to avoid types of harmful stress but also how to find the level of stress that is best for us.

There is also laboratory evidence to indicate that a certain amount of stress helps prepare an individual to withstand greater and possibly damaging levels of stress that may come later. At times stress appears to act almost like an inoculation that readies the body's defenses.

The story of overprotective parents is a familiar one. There are those parents who try to protect their children from all contact with unpleasant or stressful aspects of life. This, of course, is quite impossible. Eventually, major stresses of life do intrude into even the most well-protected lives. Not having been "immunized" to stress, the overprotected individual is unprepared emotionally, and apparently physically as well, to handle even normal stress levels. Such individuals often crumble in the face of problems that others are able to handle with relative ease.

As you can see, the implications of stress research and theory are enormous.

4

Big Problems, Little Hassles

IS IT THE MAJOR SOURCES OF STRESS IN LIFE THAT GRIND YOU down and make you feel awful, or is it the little day-to-day problems that do the most damage? Up to a few years ago, most people interested in stress concentrated on the big things. One of the most widely publicized and widely used attempts to employ stress theory to predict what will happen to an individual was the Life Events Scale. This scale or list was developed in the mid-1960s by Dr. Thomas Holmes and Dr. Richard Rahe of the University of Washington.

After interviewing and examining the health histories of several thousand people, Holmes and Rahe found what they took to be a significant relationship between major events in a person's life and his or her physical health over the next year or two. The more major changes that took place in your life, they believed, the more likely it was that you were going to be sick. It didn't make any difference whether the changes were good, like getting married, or bad, like having a member of the family die; they were all sources of stress. According to Holmes and Rahe the effect was cumulative. The more major changes in life within a year, the greater the chance of illness. The theory makes a good deal of sense in view of what we know about stress.

Holmes and Rahe even developed a 42-item table or checklist of "recent life events." They were able to assign each event a numerical value in "life-change units." Their research indicated that those who compiled more than 300 life-change units in the previous two years were more likely than others to suffer serious health problems.

The list was widely reprinted, not only in medical and scientific publications but also in newspapers and popular magazines. A lot of people were figuring out their "score." While the list was compiled specifically for adults, not teenagers, you might want to take a look at it. From it you can get a pretty good idea of what sort of events in life were considered most stressful, and just how they compared to other events:

Life Event	*Value*
1. Death of spouse	100
2. Divorce	73
3. Marital separation	65
4. Jail term	63
5. Death of close family member	63
6. Personal injury or illness	53
7. Marriage	50
8. Fired from job	47
9. Marital reconciliation	45
10. Retirement	45

Life Event	*Value*
11. Change in health of family member	44
12. Pregnancy	40
13. Sex difficulties	39
14. Gain of new family member	39
15. Business readjustment	39
16. Change in financial state	38
17. Death of close friend	37
18. Change to different line of work	36
19. Change in number of arguments with spouse	35
20. Large mortgage	31
21. Foreclosure of mortgage or loan	30
22. Change in responsibilities at work	29
23. Son or daughter leaving home	29
24. Trouble with in-laws	29
25. Outstanding personal achievement	28
26. Wife begins or stops work	26
27. Begin or end school	26
28. Change in living conditions	25
29. Revision of personal habits	24
30. Trouble with boss	23
31. Change in work hours or conditions	20
32. Change in residence	20
33. Change in schools	20
34. Change in recreation	19
35. Change in church activities	19
36. Change in social activities	18
37. Small mortgage	17
38. Change in sleeping habits	16
39. Change in number of family get-togethers	15
40. Change in eating habits	15
41. Vacation	12
42. Minor violations of law	11

The score was compiled this way: If the total number of life-change units accumulated in the last year was between 150 and 199, you were considered to be under only a moderate level of stress. With a total of 200 to 299, your stress level was medium, and with 300 units and over, stress was severe. It was at that point you faced the potential of serious health problems. You can interpret this list in terms of your own life and probably come up with an approximate life-events score of your own. Be careful, because the whole idea of big, life-changing events as the major source of stress has been undergoing substantial revision in recent years.

While you will probably still find the Holmes-Rahe list or some variation of it in most of what is written about stress even today, it's important to know that this research was really a pioneering effort. Even the list's developers acknowledged that more work was needed.

As you can see yourself, the particular events on the checklist do not necessarily apply to your life. You are, for example, probably less troubled by mortgages and more troubled by school than the people that Holmes and Rahe covered in their study. Other groups, such as single parents, the poor, minorities, and the elderly, are also not adequately covered in this list. It's not that these groups don't undergo stress; they just haven't been studied.

There is a more basic shortcoming. Simply adding up life-change units isn't enough. It tells you nothing about how an individual copes with these various changes. Thus, the statistical correlation that Holmes and Rahe found between life-events scores and illness was a fairly weak one. Something else was involved.

One problem with the early research was that the life-events approach didn't explore how these big changes are translated into the stresses of everyday life. And finally, the list concentrated only on change. It failed to take into account the stress created by chronic or repeated stressful conditions of living. Constant fighting is stressful; so is constant boredom. Isolation and loneliness can be powerful sources of stress, and so can a feeling that one is going nowhere in life. None of this can be found on the checklist of life events. Admittedly, some of these conditions are very difficult to study scientifically. But in a case where persons living together were constantly fighting, a change might actually result in lower stress.

A New Look

In an attempt to take a new look at what are the most common sources of harmful stress in our lives, Professor Richard Lazarus of the University of California and his associates tried a different approach. Instead of concentrating on the big life events, they tried to study the stressful effect produced by the little everyday problems, or the little hassles, as Lazarus calls them. They found, somewhat to their surprise, that these little hassles have an enormous effect on our mood and health. They may indeed have greater long-term effects than the big life changes.

Lazarus and his associates studied 100 subjects who agreed to fill out a variety of questionnaires over the course of the yearlong study. At the beginning and at the end of the year, they had to fill out a 24-item life-events scale. They also had to fill out monthly checklists about little hassles—things that bothered them during the course of the month. There was also an uplift checklist of things that made them feel good. In addition, there were standard questionnaires about how they felt physically and mentally, to be filled out every month.

As it turned out, it was the little hassles, the relatively petty annoyances of day-to-day life, that contributed most to feeling bad, physically and mentally. Writing in the

magazine *Psychology Today,* Lazarus said, "The more fre-
quent and intense the hassles people reported, the poorer
their overall mental and physical health." Small things do
add up. This doesn't mean that major life changes don't
produce problems. They certainly do. Sometimes the
problems don't show up until two or three years after an
event. But it was the little things that were the best predic-
tors of trouble.

The picture isn't all that simple, for big changes and
little hassles are often related. Lazarus refers to a kind of
"ripple effect" from major life changes. Here's how it
works: Let's say your parents split—a major life change
worth at least 60 life-change points on the Life Events
Scale. In addition to the big change, which is easy to see,
the split produces a situation in which there are myriad
new little problems. Suddenly there's a lot less money in
the family. You can't get that new jacket you wanted. You
have to cancel your summer travel plans. There are more
arguments with your mom over money. She's under a lot
of stress as a result of the divorce too, so her temper isn't
what it once was. Your mom gets a job and you have to do
more of the household chores than you once did. You
have less time for homework and your grades suffer. More
arguments. There are a thousand small ways in which big
changes can produce those damaging little hassles.

Attack What You Can Beat

The implications of this research for you are enormous.
They should give you hope. There are a lot of big changes
in your life that you can't do anything about. You can do
something practical about many of the little hassles that

flow from the big changes. Don't be discouraged when the big problems can't be solved. Taking care of the little hassles will do a great deal to reduce your total load of stress. And that's going to make you feel a lot better. In the example we have just given about divorce, if money seems to be a persistent source of stress, perhaps you could get a part-time job. No, it won't put your parents' marriage back together, but it might cut down on the arguing. And it will get you out of the house.

There are other hassles that result not from a life change but from a fairly stable but unhappy relationship. "Chronic role strains" are what the psychologists call them. Perhaps you really don't get along with your parents, or you genuinely hate the school that you are in. You can't change your parents. You may not even be able to change schools. But you can do something about immediate and irritating problems. The situation is not hopeless just because you can't make a big change. Try to make as many small changes as you can that will ease the sources of stress. You're going to be a lot better off.

Expecting the Unexpected

Then there are those unexpected little hassles that you really can't do anything about—the broken shoelace first thing in the morning, the lost notebook, the flat tire, the torrential rain on the night of the big dance.

In general, people who are already experiencing a great deal of stress tend to be far more affected by the unexpected hassles. It usually depends on how you happen to be feeling at the moment the unexpected arrives. What might be shrugged off and forgotten one day might set off a towering and very stressful rage on another. On that day it may be "the last straw."

Though unexpected hassles cannot always be warded off—that is the very essence of the unexpected—some problems can be anticipated. Let's say that you hate waiting in line, and crowds of shoppers drive you wild. If you know this about yourself, don't do your Christmas shopping during the Christmas rush. If you do, you're going to put yourself under a lot of unnecessary stress. Be particularly careful in trying to avoid the problems when you are already under great stress.

The Lazarus study was conducted with white, middle-class, middle-aged men and women. That group is not representative of the population as a whole. They certainly don't represent you. But what do you think was the most common source of hassle in their lives? Taxes? Investment? Crime? All these were matters of concern. But the common everyday problem that topped the list was worry about their weight! Not too far down the list were the hassles connected with a general concern about physical appearance. There are some problems that continue to bug us all through life.

What about the good things that happen to you in life? The uplifts, Lazarus and his colleagues called them; eustress, Hans Selye would call them. These can include such things as going to a great party, getting a good grade on a test, getting new clothes. Do these uplifts protect you from the negative effect of the hassles? Lazarus and his colleagues thought that they would, so they included questions about uplifts in their research. Much to the surprise of the researchers, they found the uplifts didn't seem to have any buffer effect at all. In fact, for the women in the study the uplifts seemed actually to have a negative effect upon the emotions. Many of the women felt worse when good things happened, and the men didn't feel much better.

Lazarus cautions that research in this area is still in its early stages, and it would not be wise to try to draw too many broad general conclusions. Science, it seems, has always been better at exploring the bad things that happen, rather than the good things. Doctors know a lot about disease, but even the definition of good health is elusive. Psychologists can describe a state of anxiety and depression, but happiness is a subject that has barely been studied at all. The long-term effects of these "uplifts" on stress is a subject that we obviously need to know more about.

In the meantime, this research appears to have confirmed what common sense told us a long time ago—as much as possible, get rid of the petty irritations and the little hassles in your life. These little things increase your stress load, grind you down, make you feel miserable, and ultimately could affect your health.

One of the themes we are going to return to in this book is the fact that you can't handle all of the big problems of life at once. There are some big problems that can't be handled at all. So try to take on the little problems that the big problems create, one at a time, one day at a time.

That's the kind of advice that is sometimes hard to hear. At moments you may feel that your life is falling apart, and you're being told to get a part-time job or to learn to relax your neck muscles. That sort of advice sounds as if your feelings are not being taken very seriously, and it can make you angry. But it's not that your feelings are not being taken seriously. There may simply be no practical way to attack the big problems directly. You may *have* to work on the small problems in order to gain the little victories and temporary solutions. If you remove or ease the little hassles, you will be amazed at how much less stress you will be under and how much better you will feel.

5
Parents and Family

ONE OF THE GREATEST SOURCES OF STRESS, IF NOT *THE* greatest source of stress in your life as a teenager, is your relationship with your parents. It probably won't do you much good to know that their relationship with you is one of the greatest sources of stress in their lives, too. "When you grow up and have children of your own, then you'll know what kind of heartache . . ." You have undoubtedly heard that refrain, or something very like it, many times.

You always seem to be quarreling with your parents, getting on one another's nerves, and causing one another—let's use the proper word—distress. Strangely enough, there may not be anything seriously wrong between you and your parents. A fair amount of mutual stress between parents and their teenage children is natural and inevitable. Since the stress cannot be avoided, its sources should at least be understood, and thus it may be reduced in intensity.

When you were born, your parents had all the power. You wouldn't have lasted a day if they hadn't fed you and kept you warm and protected. Parenthood, however, is a job with built-in obsolescence. Inevitably, children grow up.

Although you've been moving toward separation from your parents all your life, the teen years are critical. When you enter them you're viewed as a kid, even if you're as tall as a basketball player or as beautiful as a model. By your eighteenth birthday you can vote, drive a car, join the army—you're an adult. True, nobody ever really grows up 100 percent. Most adults have a childish side to their personality, and practically no one sheds his or her parents completely. To some extent they will always see you as their baby, and you will always view them as authority figures. In this there is the potential for a great deal of conflict and stress, and on the good side, a great deal of love and mutual support.

A lot of the conflict is necessary. If everything were smooth and pleasant, would you ever leave home? Would your parents let you take those first wobbly steps into an independent life of your own if they never felt under pressure to do so? Stress is an inherent and often positive part of the struggle to grow up.

I Want To Be Alone

When you're growing up you need more privacy than you did as a child. It gives you a sense of freedom as you start to establish your own life. But your new need for privacy can be hard for parents to handle.

Diana At fourteen, Diana, who had a good relationship with her parents when she was a child, found this out. Diana's parents just didn't see why she needed any more privacy than she did when she was a child. One day Diana came home from school to discover her mother opening a letter from her best friend at camp. Diana could hardly believe it, for her mother would never dream of opening a letter sent to another adult. Diana felt betrayed. She burst into tears and ran up to her room and slammed the door, leaving her mother with a puzzled look on her face. "She's in one of her moods again," her mother thought.

After she'd calmed down, Diana picked up the phone to call her friend Jane. She needed to complain to someone about her mother opening her mail. As Jane answered, both girls heard a click. Diana's mother was listening in on the extension.

To Diana it was a moment of crisis, but to her mother it was nothing serious. Diana confronted her mother, but it was like shouting at that famous brick wall. Diana's mother simply couldn't understand why Diana at fourteen should object to something she didn't even notice at the age of ten or eleven. Hadn't Diana's mother always kept a close eye on her daughter? Hadn't it helped make Diana feel secure? After all, she hadn't set unreasonable rules and, despite her job, had found time to join the PTA and lead a girl scout troop. She felt she had always acted like a responsible and loving parent.

Diana felt sick. It was like being socked in the stomach. You're only fourteen, her mother would say, as if she were only four. Her mother still thought of her as a child.

George   George's problem with privacy came from old family habits. His brothers and sisters entered his room whenever they felt like it. His father would give a quick knock at the door, and before George could say "Come in" his father was there. His mother, who cleaned out everybody's room from time to time, had thrown out an old sweatshirt he liked because it was stained and dirty. It sent George into a deep, silent rage. Couldn't his mother understand that at thirteen what was his was precious, inviolable, personal, and none of her damn business?

Privacy is not simply an abstract right. If you are prey to constant snooping and prying, then you are in a situation that produces chronic long-term stress. Every time your privacy is violated you will get mad, and your glands, muscles, respiration, and all the rest will react. You need a place to escape, to relax, to be by yourself. George solved his problem when he stood his ground and insisted he was old enough to have a lock for his room. It was a nuisance and inconvenient to his parents but nothing more, and they agreed to it.

Diana found that she could talk to her father more easily than her mother, so she made a choice. She could fight with her mother, each wounding the other, since Diana was not powerless—she knew how to hurt. But picking a fight and venting her feelings didn't solve much. She tried something else. At a quiet moment Diana talked to her father. She didn't sulk or attack but merely discussed her grievances. She left it to her father to handle her mother. Soon her mail was left on the hall table unopened, and she got her own phone line.

Gary   Gary wasn't so lucky. His older brother Nick had a serious drug problem, and out of desperation, his parents policed Nick's life. Because Nick hid drugs in his room, his parents would not allow a lock on Nick's door. Gary wasn't allowed to have one either.

Gary's parents imposed a set of rules on him that read like a CIA handbook. He got the endless "when I was young" line, even though as far as he was concerned dinosaurs roamed the earth when his parents were young. They invaded his inner privacy by forever asking where he was going, who he was with, how he did on the math test.

In such an atmosphere Gary was constantly tense. So, at sixteen, he did the smart thing and spent a lot of time away from home. Gary found an uncle he could talk to, as well as a few friends who would take phone calls for him. He got a part-time job to keep his mind off his family.

Change the Little Things

As Gary, Diana, and George discovered, it helps to think about ways to minimize pressure. Avoid situations that bring out the worst in your parents. Work for small, practical solutions. Don't go shopping with your mother if every time you shop you get into a fight. Be direct when you can. Tell your father not to joke around with your friends if it bothers you. Ask your mother not to hug you in a restaurant, brag about you to her friends while you're standing there, or tell stories that make you sound cute. You are not the family pet. But don't just make demands. Try to work out a reasonable compromise over when you get the family car or how often you do the dishes.

You won't be able to approach things calmly all the time, and you won't always be consistent. Nobody is, and teens of all people have days when they act like kids and days when they act like adults. George, for instance, expected his mother to vacuum his room every so often, even after he got the lock for his door. He couldn't have it both ways, and since he wanted his privacy he learned to push a vacuum cleaner himself.

If there are subjects you don't want to discuss with your parents, such as sex or how you feel about your friends, then talk to them about jobs, colleges, and other important areas that are not intimate and personal. Showing that you are willing to listen to your dad tell you how to apply for a job will keep the pressure off more explosive subjects.

You don't have to pretend to listen uncritically. Teenagers always judge their parents. Your parents' mistakes and imperfections are guideposts. You want to be different, you want to be better. But it's not very smart to think you can cut your parents out completely. You still live with them. They still have a lot of power in your life. More significantly they care about you, and they have had experiences in life you have not yet had. They don't know everything—but nobody does.

Brothers and Sisters

Brothers and sisters can cause a lot of stress between you and your parents, and they can hassle you directly. If you fought with them when you were a child, you may continue the same pattern into adolescence.

Wayne   Wayne was the second of three children. His older brother, Allan, was his father's favorite; his younger brother, Paul, was preferred by his mother. At least that's how it seemed to Wayne. He felt harassed on all sides.

The boys shared their own telephone, and Allan always

seemed to be on the phone when Wayne needed it. When Wayne tried to watch television Paul had the set monopolized. Invariably, Paul was watching some dumb little kids' show.

Paul was a whiz at math, while Wayne could barely muddle through. Allan was planning to enter premed. Wayne hadn't the foggiest idea of what he wanted to do with his life.

Things came to a head for Wayne when he was sixteen and in love with a girl named Janis. Whenever Janis came over, Allan would try to take her away from Wayne. Not only did he play up to Janis, he insulted Wayne, putting him down and making him look stupid.

One day Wayne couldn't take the pressure anymore. He began asserting himself as he never had before. He just wasn't going to be the overlooked middle child anymore. He also realized that he was old enough to break away from his brothers. Wayne spent more time away from home and avoided confrontations with Allan. Sick of being compared unfavorably to his older brother, he started meeting people who didn't even know Allan. He got a part-time job and worked full-time in the summer so he could pay for his own telephone and buy his own television set. This freed him from family fights over money. He kept the door of his room locked so Paul couldn't get in.

Allan went off to college when Wayne was seventeen. Distance improved their relationship. Wayne's moves toward independence forced his parents to deal with him in a new way. He was on the road to reducing a lot of family stress.

When Your Parents Split Up

Carolyn   At fifteen Carolyn was very critical of her parents for the mess they'd made of their marriage, for that is how she saw the breakup. There had always been strains in the family, but the period before the divorce was the worst. Her parents' marriage was like an old car that could no longer be repaired and was chugging along its last few miles.

At times like these some teens escape by adopting a substitute family. It gives them rest and comfort. Carolyn stayed at school as long as she could every day. She joined the drama club and became editor of the school newspaper. She spent her weekends hanging out with her friends. The peer group she belonged to became a kind of substitute family for Carolyn.

Divorce brings change and change is always stressful. When her parents separated at last, Carolyn and her mother moved into an apartment. Her father left town. The family's comfortable suburban house was sold. Nobody had much money. Even simple things such as where to spend Christmas and who to see on birthdays became complicated. Carolyn's emotions zigzagged. Did she side with her mother or her father? Would she have to find a new school? Would her father marry the woman he was going out with, someone Carolyn couldn't stand?

After the crisis was over, Carolyn relaxed, became more objective, and started making decisions for herself. Since her parents were happier apart, each was easier to be with. She could talk seriously to her mother for the first time in her life.

Scott and Meg   Divorce brought extra strains to Scott and Meg's lives. At first they lived with their mother. Although Meg's mother had always worked, housework had not fallen as heavily on sixteen-year-old Meg when her parents were together. Now she was stuck with cooking, cleaning, and taking care of her five-year-old brother, Ed, when her mother went out at night. In whatever spare time she had left, she had to baby-sit to pick up extra money.

Scott, seventeen, avoided housework. He ignored his sister's resentment over this, but he couldn't ignore his mother's emotional needs. She was lonely and so she leaned on Scott for psychological support. He couldn't take it, and when his father remarried, he moved in.

At first, Scott's stepmother resented him. She planned to have children of her own and wasn't happy to find herself sharing life with a seventeen-year-old boy she barely knew. They argued over the car, drinking parties, spending money, and curfew hours.

Meg, who was still with her mother, felt that she had been jammed into a slot at the edge of her mother's life. Her mother was floundering while Meg needed stability. She seemed more like a sister than a parent, worrying as much about clothes and dates as Meg did. When her mother's latest boyfriend moved in, Meg thought of quitting school and getting a job so she could move out on her own.

She decided instead to live with her grandmother for a while. They had never been close and it meant moving to another state, but it brought Meg stability after a lot of emotional warfare.

The illustrations in this chapter highlight just a few, a very few of the possible points of conflict—and thus sources of stress—between parents and children. Perhaps the problems faced by Diana, Wayne, or Meg are familiar to you. They may remind you of something that is going on between you and your own parents right now. Perhaps you have other and very different problems. It isn't the specific solutions that are important here—it's the general understanding and approach. And that is worth repeating.

1. Conflict and stress between parents and their teenage children are inevitable and, in general, necessary.

2. Repeated conflicts, arguments, and emotional upheavals lead to a situation of chronic, long-term stress, which is not only very unpleasant but can ultimately be damaging to your emotional and physical health.

3. You are not going to change your parents' view of you easily and quickly, and you are not going to change your view of them quickly and easily. So be practical and limited in your goals. Work toward the elimination of the daily aggravations, the petty irritations, the little hassles. These are what cause the bulk of day-to-day stress. Get rid of some of them and you'll feel much better.

Now there are all too many family situations in which the problems are so severe that attempts to reduce petty irritations and to get rid of little hassles aren't going to help much. They may not even be possible. A lock on the door to your room won't give you much privacy if your mother's drunken boyfriend kicks the door in.

Alcoholism, drug abuse, violence, and incest are part of everyday life for a lot of teens. Such problems are beyond the scope of this book, indeed of any book. If you face such situations in your life, don't wait around for some adult to interfere, to come and save you. And don't simply accept the situation. Go out and get help on your own. Time is not on your side with this type of problem, because if you face an utterly intolerable situation long enough, one of two things may happen. The stress of what you have been experiencing will so exhaust you that you will literally become incapable of acting on your own behalf, or you will strike out in some way that might make things even worse for you.

There are mental health clinics, crisis treatment centers, shelters for battered wives and children. Start with a guidance counselor or a social worker. (Many professionals, including teachers, doctors, and dentists, are obliged by law to report child abuse to the police. In other words, they can't ignore what you tell them. They *must* help you.) Check the phone book; go to the library. There are lawyers who can give you practical legal advice.

Some teens run away from home when things get really tough. The streets, however, are cruel and dangerous places. However, there are states where you can be declared an emancipated minor with special legal rights, if you are living in your own apartment and working. At least you have legal status and are not on the run.

To a lot of teens the stress caused by their relationship with their parents is less important than the trouble their friends give them or the problems they're having in school or on the job. After all, a lot of your life now is lived outside your home. In the next few chapters we will look at how to recognize and cope effectively with these other sources of stress.

6

Sex

WE WOULDN'T BE SURPRISED IF YOU TURNED TO THIS CHAP-
ter first.

You know where the biggest change takes place during
adolescence. It's not inside your head or in the world
around you; it's in your body itself. These changes—the
growth of body hair, menstruation and development of
breasts in girls, sperm production in boys—are caused by
changes in the production of hormones. You probably
know all about that by now. But with all the media hype
around sex and the focus on psychology, you may have to
remind yourself every once in a while that there are physical reasons for what you're going through. Remember,
stress is the body's response to any demand made upon it,
and the demands made by sexual maturation are heavy
indeed.

You can't always expect to handle life smoothly and calmly when massive changes are occurring inside you. So don't be too hard on yourself when you lose your temper and don't know why, break into tears right after you've had the giggles, or walk around depressed and gloomy for reasons you can't understand.

If there were a chart to measure stressors for teens, sex would be at the top. During adolescence it's sometimes hard to think about anything else, and no wonder. Sex is exciting, fascinating, thrilling. Orgasms enrich your life and relieve sexual tension. So if you get rid of the tension, what's the problem? Dealing with sex should be simple as ABC, right?

In the real world things don't work that way. The stress is not created solely by sexual frustration. Frustration may add to the stress, but the major causes of the stress are the physical changes that have taken place which make sex possible in the first place. These stressors exist whether you are sexually active or not.

And the sexual stressors are not just physical. You're not just a collection of chemical reactions. You're a person. Sex involves body image, self-confidence, the risk of making someone pregnant or becoming pregnant, the risk of disease, and how you feel about the other person. Sex is mental and emotional, as well as physical.

No jokes now, but sex is also social. Teens have a lot of freedom these days, although you may not always feel so free when your parents land on you with questions about who you're seeing and what you're doing. Still, compared to the way things used to be, there is a great deal of freedom. Girls don't feel they have to get married just because they're pregnant. They certainly don't have to pretend that they don't feel any sexual desires until they are married. Boys don't have to pretend they're tough and always in control. But freedom means you have to make a lot of choices on your own, and that creates a lot of stress.

Nowadays, very few parents insist that you can't date until you're sixteen or tell you that you have to be in at ten o'clock on a Saturday night. At one time there were fairly clear rules about such things. Often the rules were ignored or challenged. But for younger teens or for teens who wanted to move slowly or who needed structure, the rules helped.

Judy

Sex is inescapable. Movies, television, and commercials put you under a lot of pressure to start early. Judy, fifteen, was hypnotized by television ads that showed beautiful women in bikinis. Pictures of models with perfect faces stared up at her from the magazines she read.

Judy envied girls with big breasts and thought nobody would ever find her attractive. She wished she could trade her brown hair for blond. She became preoccupied with her appearance, hated the clothes she bought, and would decide one day that green was her color and then switch completely, refusing to wear it at all.

Actually, Judy was anything but unattractive. Her hair was pretty. Her figure was graceful. She had a pleasant smile. But in her own eyes none of this mattered. She knew only that she fell short of being ideal. Judy, who would never have become depressed over not getting straight As, succumbed to acute misery because she wasn't a grade A beauty.

Trying to measure up to an unreal standard in any area is a terrible form of pressure. Of course, that Judy would be vulnerable is only natural. Almost overnight she had grown a new body. Last year she was short. This year she was tall. Last year she still looked like a little girl; now she was turning into a woman. The process wasn't finished yet, either. This new body was still changing. Sometimes Judy had the fantasy that she was an alien being occupying somebody else's body and waiting for the real owner to come and claim it.

Judy's vulnerability made her an easy target for commercials that tell you to buy this or that lipstick or pair of blue jeans if you want to look great. She didn't realize that one reason all those people in the ads are beautiful is to make you feel insecure so you'll go out and buy the product, hoping it will make you look like a model. There's nothing wrong in wanting to look attractive, but Judy went to extremes. She confused an unattainable ideal with reality, and felt a terrible failure as a result.

Time was on Judy's side. As is often the case, Judy's physical maturity had outstripped her emotional maturity. They began to mesh after she turned seventeen. She began to notice that not all popular girls were beautiful. Some appealed to boys because they were charming, interesting, or had a strong sense of themselves.

Surfaces became less important to Judy. She got to know Leon, a shy, not particularly good-looking boy who sat next to her in homeroom. She found herself getting into deep conversations with him and discovered she really liked him. So did one of the prettiest girls in school, but Leon preferred Judy. He asked her to the senior prom. She said yes, and when she went shopping for a dress to wear to the prom she chose something on sale. This was a big breakthrough for Judy, who at one time would have had to buy the most expensive dress she could afford. She was beginning to feel secure.

Jack

It's not just girls who see only surfaces and worry about their appearance. Boys also suffer from the same insecurities. Advertising agencies know that, and they exploit it. Just see how many TV "beauty" ads are aimed at teenage boys. Jack at seventeen was overweight, but he thought of himself as a blimp. He was on the short side and well aware that even if he grew it was unlikely he would ever be tall. He had a bad case of acne and had tried every medication. Nothing worked. He figured no girl would want to go out with him, so he never bothered to ask.

As happens for a lot of teens, things really began to improve for Jack when he turned eighteen. He found out that his high marks and ability to learn easily were going to take him farther in life than some of the superpopular, good-looking boys he had graduated with. Jack went on a diet and started jogging. His complexion began to clear up on its own. He discovered that his shy, nonmacho style appealed to some of the women he met at college. Okay, he'd never dazzle anyone with his looks, but it wasn't the end of the world.

Lorraine

Lorraine's problem was different. She accepted her appearance well enough, but she felt that everything was conspiring to push her into a sexual relationship with a boy before she was ready. Magazine articles were forever telling her that sex is fun, essential to mental health, and that anyone who doesn't take the plunge is missing a lot. But Lorraine was only fourteen, and a few of her friends were sleeping with boys they found cute but otherwise didn't particularly like. Some of these relationships were messy and unhappy, with couples breaking up and going together again, fighting, and then sneaking out secretly with other people.

Lorraine wasn't sure she could cope with this intensity. She didn't even know if there was anybody she particularly liked, but her friends were urging her on. Peer pressure is tough to resist. Like a lot of teens, she wasn't at all comfortable discussing sex with her parents.

If you are in Lorraine's spot you know what emotional stress is. Though no one can decide for you what you should do, it might help you relax and ease the pressure if you think through the problem rather than act impulsively. Whether you should become sexually active or not depends on a lot of factors. Your age is a big one, and the kind of person you are is another. Physical development counts; some people mature at an earlier age than others. But be careful, because physical maturity doesn't automatically endow you with maturity in other ways. Also, if you are particularly religious or have a lot of guilt feelings about sex, it's bound to affect your attitude. Every community isn't equally free and tolerant. In some places girls can still get a bad reputation if they're considered sexually promiscuous. Abandoning the moral standards of your community can be very tough, even if you think the standards are hypocritical and wrong. Finally, you may be influenced by your parents' outlook. Will they be understanding or give you a big hassle?

If you feel just going out with one other person would

be too much of a strain, stick with a group. It's less stressful trying to get to know someone if other people are around. Your friends form a protective shield. You can kid around and be friendly, but you don't have to worry about things steaming up too much. Since teens worry a lot about how they look to their friends, you might feel you have to go out at least once in a while. Rather than put yourself under pressure, pick someone you think is nice but whom you're not wildly attracted to. If the other person feels the same, you can develop a comfortable and useful friendship.

Friends of your own sex are important, too. Then you have someone to talk to and a group to be part of, so you're not either just alone or with someone you're deeply involved with all the time. That sort of intensity can be almost too much to bear.

Let's say you've thought everything over or you're not worried about it. If you're having a sexual relationship with someone and enjoying it, fine. You're mastering one of the most important aspects of human experience. Love isn't something you have to hedge with warnings and treat as a danger. Even good sex is a source of stress, but it's eustress, the good kind, not distress, the bad kind.

What do you do about sexual excitement if you're not ready to go out? You're probably doing it already. And why not? Masturbation is a good way to learn about your body. It relieves pressure so that you don't just stare at your math book for hours seeing naked figures where the numbers ought to be. Sometimes, such as after a bout of heavy petting that doesn't go any farther, if you don't masturbate you're going to be tense for a long time.

If masturbation seems like a poor substitute for making love, don't kid yourself. Sleeping with someone doesn't automatically bring sexual satisfaction. If you're not ready or you're with the wrong person, you could have an awkward or disappointing experience. That could be a setback for you if it makes you fearful of future sexual relationships.

Sex is natural and energizing. People need it. Treat it as joyful and healthy and wait until the right moment. In the meantime, remember that even sexually active teens masturbate and have erotic fantasies. So, unless it's the compulsive focus of your life, don't worry if you masturbate and daydream.

Adam and Tanya

Approximately twelve million American teens are sexually active. What are the pressures they face? Tanya was sixteen and Adam was seventeen when they started sleeping together. They had gone out for a while and one night they just "did it." Nobody planned it. It was fun, but there were problems.

Like many teens, they thought about almost everything except the one central problem—Tanya might get pregnant. Adam knew he didn't love Tanya. Sometimes he wondered if he liked her. Tanya thought she loved Adam and then again she didn't. There was a boy in her chemistry class she longed to go out with.

Adam felt he had to seem very cool and knowledgeable about sex, which was a terrible strain. He was relieved he was no longer a virgin. His friends made fun of guys who were. He hoped he looked good with his clothes off. Tanya hoped she looked good with her clothes off. They worried about where they would meet. Tanya didn't want her parents to find out.

Sometimes they used birth control, but most of the time

they didn't. Adam bought condoms at the drugstore occasionally. When he didn't have one with him, that didn't stop them from having sex. Just as people rarely believe that they will be the one to die in a car crash if they drink and drive, so Tanya and Adam figured getting pregnant was somebody else's problem. Somehow it wouldn't happen to Tanya. They were wrong. The result was that Tanya had an abortion, which was an emotionally wrenching experience for her.

Birth Control

Making love without using birth control is gambling with the odds heavily against you. You may get away with it for a while, but sooner or later your luck will run out. If you use birth control, you may never have to cope with such stressful choices as whether to have an abortion or a baby, whether to get married, whether to give up a child for adoption. Raising a child on your own or expecting your parents to help you raise your child is a mind-boggling, life-altering decision. So is opting for marriage when you're in high school. There's no way around it: If you make love, use birth control.

There are several ways of getting the information you need. There's the library, and some health classes at school are useful, though admittedly, many are not. Many schools have a very ambiguous attitude about teaching you anything about sex. The classes tell you everything you already know and nothing you need to know.

If you are a girl, go to Planned Parenthood—it will be listed in the phone book. There are many clinics across the country. You will receive a gynecological examination, and

an appropriate method of birth control will be prescribed. You can also find out about abortion and venereal disease either from Planned Parenthood or from other clinics and hospitals. There are also private gynecologists whom you can visit. If you feel you can talk to either one of your parents or another adult about your concerns over sex, do so. If you are pregnant, an adult's help and support are essential, whether you decide to have an abortion or not. There is nothing to be gained in putting off a discussion— if you are going to have an abortion, then an early one is preferable.

Boys often think that preventing pregnancy is something for the girl to worry about. Since condoms not only protect against venereal disease but also are available at any drugstore, they are a good form of birth control.

Venereal Disease

Perhaps there is a little too much hysteria these days about venereal disease, especially herpes. It is a serious but nonfatal disease that is presently incurable. (It can be fatal to babies born to mothers with the disease, unless special precautions are taken.) Some groups have tried to use fear of venereal disease, especially herpes, to support their own traditional views of morality. Disease is viewed as a punishment for sin. The disease problem, however, can't be completely ignored. In addition to syphilis and gonorrhea, the best-known venereal diseases, urinary tract infections are something girls must watch out for. Such infections can lead to kidney ailments. Venereal diseases can cause sterility and other lifelong health problems in both boys and girls. Although many venereal diseases can be cured easily,

some, like herpes, cannot. You owe it to yourself to be alert and to find out all you can about how to protect yourself and your sexual partners from venereal disease.

Why mess up your sex life through sheer stupidity or ignorance? Avoid pregnancy and stay well. These are the two fundamental rules to follow when you become sexually active. Just about everything else you can decide for yourself.

Sexual Identity

Adolescence can be an extremely stressful time for one particular group, gay and lesbian teens. Gays worry about what their parents will say when they find out. What will other teenagers think? Often gays feel guilty and frightened, especially when they first realize that they are gay. There are also a lot of teens who worry about being gay who aren't.

When you are a teenager, being different is awful. Walk through the halls of any junior high or high school, and you'll see that people dress alike and sound alike. They're often self-conscious, worrying about how they look to others and convinced that their problems are unique.

Actually, most of the people around you share the same uncertainties, including confusion over their sexual identity. It's not odd or unnatural to be attracted to members of your own sex occasionally. If you have a good friend, someone you're close to and like, there may be times when you feel physically drawn to that person. Or perhaps it's an adult, a teacher you admire. You may never actually touch this person, but if you have fantasies about them you may become frightened and decide you are gay.

Even active sexual involvement with someone of your own sex doesn't automatically mean you are gay. For teenagers especially, sexual pressures are strong and their personalities are still forming. You are in a stage of exploration, testing and learning who you are and how your body works. This doesn't mean you shouldn't get counseling if being attracted to a member of your own sex bothers you. If you have a school psychologist you can talk to, that may be a place to start. Sometimes it's good to sort out your feelings and receive a little reassurance. Teens are quick to assume they're hopelessly weird, particularly if they veer from the conventions of their peer group.

Some people are gay. They are far more strongly attracted to members of their own sex than the opposite sex, often from an early age. High school can be extraordinarily troubling and difficult for them. Nobody wants to be insulted or teased, yet in their insecurity teens who are not gay can make life miserable for those who are. There are also parents to contend with. Some parents can accept homosexuality in their children, although usually not without anguish. Others have a much harder time; they become angry or refuse to recognize it at all.

Phil   By the time he was fifteen Phil realized he was gay. He didn't want everyone in school to know, so officially he went out with Mary. He liked her, but he had to keep a major part of his life private and hidden. He knew a few older gays, and around them he was relaxed and comfortable. He was afraid to tell his parents because he didn't like to talk about anything as personal as sex with them. Besides, he thought it might mean a big scene or major battle, with his mother in tears.

Eventually Phil told his father. At first his father refused to believe it. He felt guilty, as if he had somehow caused

Phil's homosexuality. When he realized that it wasn't a matter of blame or choice, that nobody really knows why some people are gay, he began to accept it. Phil was still his son, still had the same mix of strengths and weaknesses. Why turn against him just because of one facet of his entire being?

Phil talked things over with his father, and both agreed it would be best not to tell his mother yet, perhaps not until Phil was older and on his own. Phil also felt he could not "come out of the closet" around his high-school friends. His father agreed, understanding that Phil had to decide for himself where it was safe to be openly gay. He did suggest that Phil might want to join a gay discussion group to receive support and advice. There are many such groups and they provide counseling and assistance. Phil located one through his older gay friends, and it made a big difference in his life. He stopped going out with Mary, which freed her to find someone who really wanted to be with her, and he made friends with a couple of gay teens at school.

Society is no longer as cruel to gays as it once was. The laws are fairer and a lot of people have changed their attitudes. Gays are no longer routinely considered sick or sinful. Although still highly stressful, the awareness that you are gay doesn't have to destroy your life and blight your future.

Quite the opposite! Gay sex can be as satisfying as any other form of sex. Like Phil you can find gay lovers and friends even while going to a conventional kind of high school.

For everybody, gay or straight, just as one's relationship with one's parents often improves after adolescence, so does sex become easier to cope with. People become more secure, less self-absorbed, and as a result, they become less preoccupied with their personal appearance.

You may want to wait until you reach that level of security before becoming sexually involved with someone. It's okay to say no. But you don't have to impose that kind of restraint and frustration upon yourself if you don't want to. Nobody has to tell teenagers that there's a lot of pleasure in sex.

7

School and Other Kids

IN HIGH SCHOOL THE COMPETITION FOR GRADES TURNS deadly serious, especially for teens headed for college. Teachers put you under pressure to achieve, and parents reinforce them. You may feel at times that to your parents you're nothing but a vehicle for their ambitions, that you're expected to be some kind of studying machine. Yet with so many other things on your mind, it's even harder to concentrate than it was when you were in fifth grade. For some, the stress of trying to maintain high academic achievement can be overwhelming. Some teens have been known to crack under the load. Most people, however, manage to survive pretty well.

Mike

Mike was an A student right through junior high. He was quiet and obedient as a child, but in his first year of high school he began to feel stifled. His parents were very judgmental about swearing, smoking, and even the faintest possibility that Mike might want to go out with a girl. Mike knew that separating himself from his parents was going to be a battle.

A good part of the reason for Mike's As was that he had always been neat and conscientious, the kind of student who doesn't give his teachers any trouble. Quiet and obedient students often have the advantage in grades. Mike began to rebel a bit by asking challenging questions and daydreaming about girls when he was in a particularly boring class. Once he was home, he'd sometimes skip doing homework if he became absorbed in an interesting book. When he brought home his report card, his parents became extremely upset. Not that his marks were bad, but Mike was no longer in the top 15 percent of his class. He was grounded by his parents and told to bring his marks up.

Mike wasn't lazy or indifferent. He just couldn't work any harder at this point of his life, because that would have meant devoting every available moment and every ounce of his energy to study and academics. What his parents didn't see was that Mike was thinking critically and independently for the first time in his life, both in and out of class. He was also learning to handle stress, escaping into a book when he'd had a rough day or reaching out to make friends.

Like a lot of shy people who have never broken the

rules, he was drawn to risk-taking rebels, the bold and out-spoken, but he rarely emulated them. Once, he got caught smoking marijuana in his room, and his parents panicked. But Mike was no drug addict. He was an ordinary teen-ager experimenting, testing, finding out about life. There was no real cause for panic, but Mike's parents had yet to come to terms with reality. They had to learn that Mike was a person, not an ideal.

The pressure to be a top student can be cutthroat and brutal. If you believe that anything less than Harvard or Yale dooms you to failure, then you are subjecting your-self or being subjected to excessive stress. There are peo-ple who breeze into the school of their choice and others who work hard to make it. However, if you feel your life will be over if you don't have a high score on your SATs or if you collapse every time you bomb out on a chemistry exam, then it's time to ease off.

Lenore

Lenore went to a big suburban high school where the atmosphere was highly competitive. Parents drew a lot of self-esteem from where their kids were going to college. To be fair, they also wanted the best for their children and hoped to give them every advantage. Lenore was a good student when it came to verbal subjects like English, but math was difficult for her. She was an outgoing girl with a pleasing personality who had lots of friends. She was a fairly talented artist, liked to ride horses, and although she had no clear idea what she'd like to do with her life, at sixteen she had plenty of time to find out.

If her parents had accepted her the way she was or if her

teachers had been more relaxed, Lenore would have been a reasonably happy person, able to cope well with the normal ups and downs of adolescence. But she always seemed to be a disappointment. Though her parents never expressed it in those terms, Lenore could sense what they really felt. She tried hard in math, but for all her efforts she got Cs while some of her friends got Bs and others As with half the effort. Her science marks were mediocre, not because she failed to do her homework, but because she just didn't seem to be able to organize the material adequately. She wasn't neat and she wasn't orderly. Yet when her other subjects were averaged in, her grade average put her comfortably in the top half of her class.

She never felt or was allowed to feel that this was enough. The pressure of endlessly falling short got to Lenore. She made friends with Joe, a bright boy who responded to pressure by giving up. He was close to dropping out of school. Lenore didn't want that to happen to her, but she was deathly scared of the SATs. She'd been taking a preparatory course to help her get a high score, but the course only made her more anxious. She wondered if Joe was right, if she should quit school. Maybe she should get on a bus and go to New York City, and get a job. As the SATs grew closer, Lenore thought more and more about running away.

Luckily, a new guidance counselor came to Lenore's high school. Lenore talked to him about the pressure she was under. He helped her see the good things about herself, pointing out that an ability to get along well with people is one of the most important talents you can have. He reminded her that people with straight As mess up, too, that life is unpredictable, and that being at the top of your class, though useful, is not an automatic ticket to success later. He encouraged Lenore to take more art courses and to start thinking of college in terms of her own needs. Where would she be happiest?

Lenore could now face the tests she had to take. Her scores were adequate but not brilliant. She found she could live with that and even cope with her parents' disappointment. Although she continued doing her homework regularly, she stopped beating her head against the wall and accepted getting Cs in some subjects. This gave her more time for her favorite hobby, horses. She started riding lessons again and won a blue ribbon at a horse show.

On Being Unpopular

A lot of people with top grades would probably trade places with Lenore if they could, because school is not only academic pressure but peer pressure as well. Peer pressure is jargon for the pressure you feel from other kids. Though Lenore had an easy time making friends, many teens do not. If tests are stressful, what's a snub? If putting up with a teacher who gives you a hard time is bad, being unpopular can be much worse. For one thing, your parents can request an interview with a teacher or guidance counselor if you have trouble in school. Sometimes that resolves a problem. When it comes to the other kids, the situation is a lot tougher. In adolescence you may feel alone, isolated, and different to a degree that you will never experience again. As we have seen, all of these feelings create enormous stress. It can make you feel so bad that you can barely function.

Teenagers just naturally form cliques. When you were a little kid you may have been a brownie or cub scout or a member of some other children's organization. Generally, membership in these groups is open to anyone and is controlled by adults. A clique is different. The very essence of a clique is exclusivity. It provides members with shelter. You're not just out there braving the wilds of high school alone. You belong; you have friends; you have a place. For those who are part of a clique, particularly a popular one, that can be very reassuring. Unfortunately, cliques also draw part of their power from dismissing outsiders and putting them down.

Obviously, the pressure is greatest on those who are excluded, but even if you are at the core of the top clique you will not escape pressure. Cliques tend to enforce conformity. You have to dress a certain way and think a certain way or at least pretend to, in order to belong. If you are a member of a top clique, you know that there's a lot of rivalry and competition within the group that isn't seen by those on the outside.

Since there are only a few superpopular people in any school, most teens have to deal with the stress of being on the outside looking in. You may feel jealous, angry, unappreciated, and misunderstood by your peers. Though you can't wish away the top clique, your best bet is to form a group of your own. Even a few friends can make a big difference.

Extracurricular organizations are usually more open than the cliques teens form themselves. If you have a particular interest or talent, joining a school club will help you find others like yourself. There are debating teams, math teams, cheerleaders, drama clubs, science clubs, bands and choral groups, computer clubs, audiovisual clubs, the school newspaper, yearbook, service clubs, and lots more. There are cliques even within such groups, but they are usually not as rigid as social cliques.

Another release from the stress caused by peer pressure

is to keep channels open to the world beyond school. As teens get older, they usually move in this direction, anyway. They get part-time jobs if they can find them. They start thinking about college, the military, special job training programs—all sorts of possibilities of life beyond high school. But you don't have to wait until your senior year in high school. If you've been focusing too much on the social scene at your high school, cool it by checking out community centers, noncredit courses at a nearby college, or any place that offers special programs for teens. There are summer camps for teens, amateur theater groups, hobby centers, gyms and recreational facilities. You'll meet a new group of people and gain a different perspective on school.

If you like to be alone and don't want to join a group, that's fine. Maybe you're the kind of person who prefers to have one or two close friends to being part of a crowd. If you have no friends at all or really feel lost socially, then you should talk to an adult you like and trust.

Some teens have a lonely time in high school because of the kind of school they go to. Going to a big school that has a lot of violence or racial tension is very different from a small private school. If you are musically gifted and attend school where there's a strong music program, you'll probably make friends. However, if you put the same person in a vocational school they may feel isolated.

If there seems to be any sure road to popularity, especially for boys, it's athletics. Most schools large or small, city or suburban, emphasize sports. You will rarely find the star of the football or basketball team hurting for recognition. Does that mean there's no anxiety attached to sports? Of course not. As a matter of fact, sports are an enormous source of stress, for many teens the focus of far more anxiety than academics.

The stress starts as early as Little League when parents start boasting about their sons' athletic prowess. By the time a boy's in high school, his family may expect him not only to make the team but to excel. Being a high-school athletic hero means instant glory. Schools usually display trophies and plaques prominently. Local papers give more coverage to high-school sports than any other high-school activity. In most cases, the pressure on girls to excel in sports is not as great. So it is the boys who are usually the victims of an overemphasis on sports.

Alan   Alan's case is typical. He wanted to please his father, who was a big sports fan, but Alan was a mediocre athlete. He lacked the strength and coordination necessary for team sports. When he received a minor injury in a football game, it gave him the excuse he needed to quit. Although he was mildly depressed for a while, he got over it and developed new interests. He didn't abandon sports. Eventually he took up running for pleasure, not in competition. He enjoyed it and found the exercise relaxed him and helped him keep in shape. Sports became a release from stress rather than a cause of it. On autumn Saturdays you'll find Alan absorbed in watching a football game, an activity he enjoys much more than playing the game.

Vince   Vince, on the other hand, was a gifted athlete who loved all kinds of sports. He could handle the pressures of high-school athletic competition. But when he realized he had a shot at professional sports, he began getting headaches. Everyone was at him, urging him to work harder, become stronger, push himself to achieve more. He couldn't face making mistakes. He felt burdened by his responsibilities. For Vince the stress had become too great.

One night he started drinking, got into the family car,

and drove like a maniac. There was an accident. Vince was okay but the car was totaled. When his parents talked to him about it, he burst into tears. Vince went into therapy. He accepted his limitations, scaled down his goals, and is planning to become a physical education teacher if he can't make it as a professional. That's an idea he's comfortable with. At least he no longer feels he has to be a superstar or life isn't worth living.

Risk Taking

Speeding, as Vince did, is a common teenage response to stress. Teens are risk-takers, anyway. You can't find out who you are if you don't try new things. But there's more to it than self-discovery. Teens generally smoke, drink, and try drugs because of peer pressure. If your friends do something, no matter how much you may want to say no, it's hard to find the strength to resist. It's hard to be different. It's uncomfortable to feel that you may be missing out.

Drinking usually produces less stress than drugs, but it is not necessarily any less dangerous. The physical effects of alcohol can be just as severe as those of most drugs. The reason drinking is less stressful is simple—we are a drinking society. Although some parents smoke pot or take heavy drugs, most don't. Almost all adults have at least an occasional drink, and a lot of kids have parents who are heavy drinkers.

Parents who panic if they catch their children smoking a joint take teenage drinking parties in stride. Although alcohol is supposed to be off limits for teens it's easy enough to get, and the laws governing drinking are mild compared to the laws on the books about drugs. You may be refused a drink in a bar, but you are probably not going to wind up in jail for trying to get one.

Except for driving when drunk or speeding at any time, most risk-taking behavior isn't fatal, if you don't overdo it. But adolescence is not a time of life when moderation is easy to achieve. If you feel that you've got to drink or take drugs to escape stress, then you're on the road to real trouble. If without it you and your friends wouldn't know how to pass the time, then you'd better start looking for alternatives.

Remember, stress isn't all bad. Running away from stress at all costs can be hazardous to your life and health. Alcohol and other drugs are themselves stressors. There are safer and more effective ways of lightening your stress load, and we will discuss some of them later on.

Religion

Religion holds an important, even a central place in the lives of many teens. But for many others, perhaps most others, religion is something abstract and distant, something that does not affect their daily lives.

A lot of people insist that religion is good for you because it gives you strong values that help you cope with the stress of your teenage years. That can be true, but when religious values come in conflict with the attitude of your peers, they can become a major source of stress.

Andrea   Andrea had grown up in a moderately religious family, but she had always felt that she was "more religious" than her parents, and when she was fifteen she joined a very active church youth group. The members of this group took their religion very seriously. Drinking, smoking, and sexual activity were not only frowned upon but were condemned as absolutely sinful. Rock music and R-rated movies were also on the forbidden list. Andrea made a lot of friends in her youth group, but the more she adopted the attitudes of the group, the harder things became for her at school.

Her old friends, the ones she had known before she joined the youth group, teased her for being a prude who thought she was better than other people. Even kids she didn't know made fun of her for wearing a pin that said "Love Jesus" to school. Andrea began to dread school and to wish that she could spend all her time with the youth group. But Andrea lived in a large city where most people did not share her views. Her parents, who were made quite uncomfortable by Andrea's religious activities, insisted that she remain in public school.

It took a few sessions with one of the school guidance counselors to help Andrea see what could be done to ease this strain. Her religious views were her own business. If she didn't want to smoke or drink, and if she disapproved of premarital sex, that was her business. But trying to push her ideas on others around her was tactless, futile, and probably counterproductive. It made her seem harsh and judgmental, and invited hostility from her classmates. Andrea found it was a lot smarter to share her views only with those who would be receptive to them, or at least would understand them. Once she stopped coming on so strong, her life ran more smoothly.

Cults It's not always that easy. Sometimes involvement in religion can completely isolate a person from friends, family, from the whole world that he or she used to know. Here we are talking specifically about the religious cults that have attracted so much attention over the last few years.

While it is true that many of the stories that appear in the press or on television about cults are sensationalized, and that the number of teens who become deeply involved with cults is very small, it is also true that teenagers are the ones most attracted to religious cults. The reasons are not hard to find. They are what we have been talking about all along—all the pressures, all the changes, all the stress of this time of your life.

Worried about friends and family? A cult seems to supply both. Worried about morals and values? The cult says it has all the answers. Worried about what you are going to do with your life? The cult will tell you. Worried about making all kinds of decisions? Worry no more; in a cult the decisions are made for you.

Joining a cult can provide at least a temporary release from stress. But you pay a big price—you give up all your autonomy, all your freedom, mental and physical. And you run a big risk, because you may be putting your life in the hands of a crook or a madman. Many cult leaders have been one or the other, or both.

Even if the cult is, from top to bottom, made up of sincere, dedicated and honest people, by joining you are still cutting yourself off from the rest of the world. The fact is that the vast majority of teens who join cults don't stay with them for more than a few weeks or months. Cults are very reluctant to discuss the rate of defection, but it's tremendous. In most groups it runs seventy or eighty percent. Reentry into the world after the cult experience is tough.

Making a deep religious commitment is not the sort of thing that should be done quickly. Remember that there are moments in your life when you may find yourself extremely vulnerable to the cult appeal. If the cult really does have the handle on Absolute Truth, then that Truth will be there next year. You can afford to wait and think about it.

8

The Weather, Nuclear War, and Other Sources of Stress

SO FAR WE HAVE BEEN DISCUSSING SOME OF THE BIG AND dramatic sources of stress, or stressors, in your life. Generally these are emotional, mental, and social in nature. But remember our original definition of stress as the body's general response to *any* stimulus. Obviously there are an awful lot of things in the world that can produce stress in you. In emphasizing life events and the emotions as sources of stress (which they most certainly are), we may tend to overlook some of the others. This can lead to confusion over how much stress we undergo every day.

Hans Selye, the father of modern stress research, spent most of his long career doing research on the stress created by such things as toxic chemicals and low temperatures. All too often we ignore such stressors. Let us correct the error and look at some of these sources of stress in our own lives.

The Weather

Inevitably, we come up against the hoary old saying that everyone talks about the weather but no one does anything about it. True enough. And you may wonder why it is necessary to discuss a source of stress that you can't do anything about. While you cannot change the weather, you must at least take it into account. You have to know how it affects you.

We repeat: Stress is cumulative; it builds up. In their book on stress management, *The Stress Management Workbook,* Dr. Stephen Aronson and Dr. Michael F. Mascia compare human stress tolerance to the action of a pickup truck. A truck may be designed to carry a one-ton load without damage. It could also carry a load of a ton and a half at slow speed over level ground. But if the driver tries to push that overloaded truck over rough ground or up a hill, there is the risk of serious damage. Thus, if you add the stress caused by extreme weather to all of the other stressors in your daily life, you may soon find yourself at the point where you are unable to cope with the day.

It has been known for centuries that weather has a profound effect on how we feel. There have been a large number of scientific studies done on stress and certain types of weather, particularly the hot dry winds known in Europe and America as the *sirocco* and *Föhn,* in Africa as the *khamsin* or *sharkiye,* and in Israel as the *sharav.*

In certain individuals these winds produce a range of psychological and physiological changes from headaches and sharp mood shifts to a loss of sodium in the body and changes in hormone balance. From time to time the effects of these winds have even been taken into account by the legal system. People who have committed crimes during periods when these winds were blowing have been successful in claiming diminished responsibility because of the winds. During periods when the sirocco blows, practically everyone becomes aggressive and irritable.

We all know that we feel better on bright sunny days than on dark gloomy ones, and that both extreme cold and extreme heat make us feel tired. Heat and cold are known stressors. We are not sure why sunlight affects us, but it does.

Some recent studies have shown that the amount of sunlight some depressed persons are exposed to has a direct effect upon their state of mind. The more sunlight, the less depressed they feel. In the northern hemisphere, most of us simply feel better in mid-June than in mid-January. Practically every living creature responds to light in many important ways. There's no reason why we should be any different.

Repeated experiments have shown that cold and damp weather by itself does not give you a cold or the flu. You get such diseases from exposure to viruses or bacteria. But apparently the general stress created by the cold damp weather lowers the body's resistance to diseases, and that is one of the reasons why we tend to get more colds, cases of the flu, and similar illnesses in the winter.

Temperature and sunlight are just the obvious meteorologic factors that affect us. There is considerable scientific evidence to indicate that there are a host of additional more subtle influences as well. The ionization of the air appears to have an effect upon the mood of many people. The earth's magnetism, solar eruptions, and cosmic rays have also been implicated as having some stressor effect. But here we are admittedly entering a highly speculative realm.

What all of this indicates is that there may be, and probably are, powerful stressors all around you that you are not even aware of. Some of your mood swings and feelings of fatigue are profoundly influenced by factors outside of your body rather than inside your head.

Time

The invention of the electric light has blurred the once sharp distinctions between night and day. The relatively modern inventions of heating and air conditioning have taken the edge off the change of seasons. But we are living in bodies that are still adapted to the rhythms of day and night and the change of seasons. Human beings have been ruled by these rhythms for millions of years. They are part of our biological heritage.

Research over the last two decades has proved overwhelmingly that our bodily functions operate on a regular rhythmic schedule. Temperature, blood pressure, heart rate, brain wave rhythm, body chemistry—virtually every bodily function ebbs and flows in a pattern over the course of a day, a week, a month, a year. The patterns are often complicated and interlock with one another, but they are there.

Even disease seems to have its rhythm. Experiments have shown that the severity of the reactions of allergic people tends to vary over the course of a day. When you have a cold or other virus, you know that at certain times of the day you feel better than at other times. In most virus diseases, your temperature goes up and down in a regular way, quite unaffected by aspirin or any other medical intervention.

Moods certainly vary. What seems overwhelming at two in the morning may be nothing more than a minor difficulty by eleven o'clock. Certain foods eaten at one time of day will be digested with ease. At another time the very same food will cause severe indigestion. We are able to learn better at certain times of day than at others.

Long-distance travel disrupts the regular rhythms of the body and produces the phenomenon known as jet lag. Repeated studies of night workers and, more significantly, individuals who work different shifts—night one week, day the next—have proved that this sort of work can produce serious consequences. Workers who have had too many changes of shift become irritable, inefficient, and accident prone. They complain more, get sick more, and work less efficiently than those on regular shifts. They suffer from insomnia, indigestion, and mental confusion. In short, they show all of the symptoms of excessive stress.

For better or worse, the world we live in is ruled not by the rhythms of our body but by the clock and the calendar. It may be that your mind works best at four in the afternoon, but your toughest class is your first at eight o'clock, when you feel barely alive. There are periods when you have to drive yourself, even though the natural rhythms of your body are being overridden and ignored.

But you can't do it all the time. If you try, you are risking serious consequences in terms of mental and physical ill-health.

Air and Water Pollution

We know that toxic chemicals can be powerful stressors even when they don't kill you or make you ill immediately. We also know that over the past twenty or thirty years a huge number of possibly toxic chemicals have been introduced into our environment. What we do not really know yet is the effects that these chemicals may be having on us.

Certainly we know the dramatic effects—evil-smelling smog that causes our throats to go dry and our eyes to burn, and that can kill people with respiratory diseases. Exhaust fumes give us a headache and nausea. Undrinkable water may be laced with cancer-causing chemicals. But we are talking about stress, a general condition, one that is often difficult to measure or even recognize. What are the long-term stressor effects of air and water pollution? The scary fact is that we simply don't know. In the study of the effects of these various chemical agents, medical science is about where it was in the study of infectious disease, when Louis Pasteur first presented his theory of microorganisms over a century ago. Stress research has a long way to go in this area.

Likewise, the health effects of high doses of radiation are well known. It can kill you outright or give you cancer. However, radiation, like chemical agents, is a powerful stressor. What are the long-term stress effects of even low "safe" levels of radiation? Once again, the scary and unsatisfying answer is that we don't know.

Food

For most of the history of the human race, indeed for most people in the world today, the overpowering danger in connection with food is not being able to get enough of it. For most of us in America today, that is not the danger. Indeed, the real danger is getting too much food or not the right kind.

Dieting is an American obsession, particularly with teens. The extreme of dieting is the now well-publicized eating disorder anorexia nervosa, in which an individual literally starves herself (most victims are women) to death. This is a serious condition, one that usually requires professional help and a long period of convalescence.

Any diet or radical change in eating patterns creates a great deal of stress. If you have ever been on a diet (and who hasn't), you know that even a very moderate one can make you feel depressed, irritable, and fatigued.

Don't take dieting too casually. It can be a very powerful stressor. Stay away from extreme diets; be sure that you are getting enough calories to run your body properly, and that your diet is well balanced. Most well-planned diets will provide sufficient calories, vitamins, and minerals. Even so, there is plenty of stress.

Dieting requires a change in some of your most fundamental habits—your eating habits. While you may have enough calories to keep you going, you are probably going to have dramatic reductions in certain types of foods— sugar, for example. This all requires adaptation to change, and change equals stress.

The same can be said for weight gain. Weight gain involves body changes, and that results in stress.

There are certain foods that are known to create stress. Most medical attention has been focused on caffeine-containing stimulants such as coffee, tea, and cola drinks, which among other things increase your pulse rate. But we all have particular foods that "disagree" with us and thus create stress.

This is an area in which you do have some control. If a diet is putting you under excessive stress—stop. Or at least modify the diet. Being thin isn't everything, and it's nothing if you're miserable. Find a diet you can live with and a weight you can live with. Your whole quality of life may be better if you weigh a few pounds more than your ideal weight.

If you think that coffee or cola is having a bad effect on your nervous system, cut back. In fact, if you habitually drink a lot of coffee or cola, cut back anyway and see if you feel better for it. But keep in mind that caffeine appears to be slightly addictive, and cutting back can produce mild withdrawal symptoms, such as headaches, in some individuals. These symptoms disappear as the body adjusts to the lower level of caffeine.

Smoking, Drinking, and Drugs

It is hardly necessary to run down the list of dangers involved in smoking, drinking, or taking drugs. You've heard it all before. It is useful, however, to point out that all of these practices have general stress effects, in addition to their well-known specific effects. Often when a person is in a highly stressful situation, he or she will tend to smoke more heavily, drink, or turn to drugs as a relief from the stress. Ironically, such stress "relief" may actually increase the stress load.

Aside from illicit or recreational drugs such as marijuana or cocaine, there are lots of prescription drugs—medicines—that we take from time to time. They are taken to cure a particular disease or alleviate a specific symptom such as pain. These, too, act as powerful stressors on the body, and many have severe side effects. The more powerful the drug, the greater the stress.

The obvious solution—don't drink or take drugs to relieve stress.

Disease and Injury

Once again it seems almost unnecessary to say that disease or injury causes stress. Quite obviously they do. But while we often pay close attention to the specific effects of illness or injury, we tend to overlook the stress it creates. We may think that once the specific symptoms have disappeared, or once the wound has healed, we are just fine. But we aren't. One of the first things that stress researchers discovered was that the stress of illness hangs on long after all the specific signs of the illness itself have disappeared.

Crowding and Noise

One of the most dramatic events in the animal world is the "migration" of lemmings to the sea. Every few years millions of these little northern rodents will begin what appears to be a mass migration toward the ocean. Along the way most are eaten by predators or killed in other ways. They seem to plunge suicidally into streams and rivers, and finally into the ocean. They are not really determined to kill themselves; they just don't realize how far they have to swim.

For a long time people believed that the lemmings were driven by starvation. Closer examination has shown that they live in areas in which there is plenty of food before they begin their migration. It now appears that the reason for the migration is that the lemming population rises and falls regularly. When it rises beyond a certain critical point, the lemmings are driven to migrate by the stress created by crowding.

In one way or another the same sort of behavior has been observed among many other kinds of animals. Deer living in dense populations will fall prey to disease, and rats living crowded together will become extremely aggressive or relapse into an almost catatonic state. This is all the result of the stress caused by crowding.

What happens to lemmings, deer, and rats also happens to human beings, at least to some extent. The effects of crowding on stress have been studied extensively. The conclusion that has come out of these studies is that while crowding does indeed produce stress, the relationship is not a simple one.

The big city is everybody's idea of a crowded and stressful environment. Yet a teenager in the city may live in a large apartment with no brothers and sisters, and plenty of personal space. A farm kid may be surrounded by acres of wheat, but he or she may have to share a bedroom with three others. Which person is more likely to suffer from the stress of crowding? A small home where everybody's individual privacy is rigidly respected may feel less crowded than a large one where people are always barging in on one another. Still, there can be no doubt that a morning spent riding a jammed train or bus is a stressful morning indeed.

Noise can be a touchy subject for teens. While there is no doubt that noise does cause stress—and ultimately can cause hearing loss—we all tolerate different levels of noise. Music so loud that it would send most parents to bed with a raging headache is considered routine and pleasurable by many teenagers. The noise and crowding of a rock concert seem intolerable to most adults, while most teens find them simply exciting. Once again we must remind you that the stress is there, even if the situation is an enjoyable one.

Isolation and Boredom

First you have to worry about crowds; now we tell you to worry about being alone. Sorry, but that's the way it is with stress; you just can't win. Extreme isolation is one of the most stressful situations imaginable.

Experiments with laboratory animals, particularly social animals like rats and mice, show that the animals rapidly begin to display all the symptoms of extreme stress when kept in isolation. There are rapid and dramatic changes in the body chemistry as well as major alterations in behavior. Introduce another mouse or two into the cage, and the body of the once-isolated mouse quickly returns to normal.

Studies of prisoners who have been kept in solitary confinement show the same sort of rapid and dramatic changes. Sometimes this can produce not only physical illness, but symptoms which resemble extreme mental illness. If the isolation goes on long enough, it may result in real and permanent mental damage. Isolation, sleep deprivation, and noise form the basis of the behavior modification techniques that have been called brainwashing or programming.

Most of us are not living in solitary confinement or anything like it. Being alone for a while is good for everyone. But prolonged social isolation is highly stressful. Isolation is often related to boredom. This, too, can be a source of considerable stress. Normal functioning for the brain and body depend on a certain level of continuous sensory input. Cut down the level below a critical point, and brain and body cease to function properly.

The sensory deprivation experiments represent an extreme laboratory example. Volunteers float for hours or days in tanks of warm water. They are in a totally dark environment, with all outside sound masked by "white noise," any soft, steady noise like a hum. At first many found the experiments relaxing—but very quickly they could become horrifying. The subjects would become depressed, frightened, and often experience startling hallucinations.

Hans Selye found this very significant in terms of stress theory. He wrote, "As we have so often said, living beings are constructed for work, and if they have no outlet for their pent-up energy, they must make extreme efforts at adaptation to this unphysiologic state of inactivity." That state has even been given a name—deprivation stress.

Of course we do not spend our lives floating in tanks of warm water. But we do go through long periods of monotony, where we are not getting adequate sensory input. The phonograph or the TV may be on, the teacher may be talking, but all of this can be little more than the everyday equivalent of the white noise used in sensory deprivation experiments.

Yes, boredom is as stressful as excitement, sometimes more so. At the end of a long, boring day we may feel more exhausted than if we had been running about for hours.

Zeitgeist

Zeitgeist is a German word that means the spirit of the age or the general atmosphere of the times—the way most people feel, what they believe, what they hope and what they fear. There is no exact equivalent in English for this useful term, and so some sociologists and historians have adopted the German term.

Well, the zeitgeist, the spirit of our age, has its effects upon all of us. It is yet another stressor. The one overpowering fact of the modern zeitgeist is that we all know that we live in the nuclear age, and right now we possess the technology to exterminate our own species. We also do not possess, in any great measure, enough faith in the rationality or innate goodness of the human species that would lead us to believe that it would be impossible for us to blow the hell out of ourselves at any time. In fact, an awful lot of us feel that this is what will happen.

Even when there is no immediate war threat on the horizon, and the nightly news is not particularly alarming, the knowledge that our world could be destroyed if just a few people pushed a few buttons is not comforting. Indeed, it is highly stressful. How stressful no one knows for sure. It is not the sort of stress that can be measured. Some, like Yale psychologist Robert Jay Lifton, have argued that the psychic toll of such knowledge is immense.

It isn't just nuclear war and the threat of total destruction. We worry about unemployment, our own or our parents', making ends meet, social injustice, a clouded and uncertain future, and much more.

We do not live in a wildly optimistic or idealistic age. The zeitgeist of the 1980s is rather gloomy. By and large, however, young people are much more optimistic and idealistic than their elders. We suspect that this is an absolute biological necessity. If young people automatically adopted the same gloomy narrow and "practical" views so often espoused by the adults around them, our species would probably still be living in caves. We would never have tried to do anything better.

Well, that's quite a list of stressors—everything from today's weather to the fear of nuclear war. And as we said, you can't do anything about the weather. But you can do something about nuclear war. No, you can't stop nuclear war all by yourself, but if it is a problem that concerns you, or if there are other problems in the world around you that you find extremely disturbing—toxic wastes, poverty, or whatever—find an organization that is working on the problem and get involved. Do something. Being active in a constructive way is much less stressful than sitting around and brooding. It's a good cure for the stress of boredom. It's a marvelous outlet for the energy of youth. And you might do a lot of good in the world. Remember, the world really is changed by the young.

But there is still the weather and some other things that you can't do anything about. You can't even join an organization that is out to change the weather. Why bother to go over such subjects? There's a good reason. It is to make you aware of the many, many sources of stress in your life. Even if you can't do anything about a particular stressor, if you know it's there you are ahead of the game. The knowledge that boredom or extremes of weather are highly stressful will help you understand the way you feel sometimes. It will also help you plan your stress load. Don't take on a new and difficult task at a time of day when your energy is already low. The feeling of fatigue that you have at the end of a day in which you have done nothing does not mean that you are physically tired and therefore should do less. It may mean just the opposite.

It's important to realize that your ups and downs are not all in your head—that out there in the real world there are real sources of stress which press in upon you, often when you are not even aware of them.

9
The Breaking Point

HAVE YOU EVER THOUGHT ABOUT COMMITTING SUICIDE?

Adults often find the idea of suicide so frightening they switch off when teens even try to talk about the subject. Yet, teens do kill themselves—five thousand a year in America alone. And many more try it. In the overall population the ratio of attempted suicides to actual suicides is estimated to be around 10 to 1. In the high-school-age population the ratio is about 100 to 200 to 1.

Perhaps if adults listened, really listened to the words of some of the songs most popular with kids today, they might understand how the kids sometimes feel. A host of popular groups have all had songs that speak of being at the breaking point. This music appeals to those who sometimes feel that they have got too much to handle. It's popular because it expresses what kids are thinking. There is a lot of very serious unhappiness out there.

So you're not alone, weird, or crazy if you feel so overwhelmed at times that dying seems like the only way out from under the load. You go from down in the depths of depression to stratospheric highs. Every day is mined with threats. You have to make adult decisions, and all you can bring to them are years of childhood and a short span of adolescence. In a sense, everything is brand new.

Newness means change and mood shifts and inherent instability. By now you have learned enough about stress to see where that leaves you. The great nineteenth-century sociologist Emile Durkheim was one of the first to study suicide. His work led him to conclude that suicide rises with instability. Change, whether good or bad, can drive some people to kill themselves. And who changes more than teenagers? That is why suicide is the third leading cause of death among teenagers. Tell that to the next adult who says "these are the best years of your life," and "teenagers don't know what real worries are."

A lot of adults romanticize youth, both yours and their own. Selective memory has made them view their own teens as rosier than they were. They don't remember how charged and anxious even the up times were. What would they say about Freddie Prinze, the young comedian who shot himself after he made it big? In short they don't remember how stressful it is to be young. And they refuse to admit, sometimes, until it is too late, that the load can be overwhelming for some.

Who is to say what makes for crushing stress? At one time in your life your parents were gods. There were some certainties in life. Now you are painfully aware of your parents' faults and limitations. Big questions about what to do with your life merge with more immediate problems:

Should I go on a diet, try for the team, break up with my boyfriend? Do I look awful in blue? If I wear these clothes, will I make a fool of myself? You're critical of your body. You want to look so much better than you do. You're sure everybody else notices everything wrong with you.

There are a number of theories about what causes suicide, and many of them are contradictory. We're not sure that when you're at the point of feeling you want to kill yourself, familiarity with one theory or another is going to do you much good. The only thing that matters is keeping you alive, because things are going to get better.

Let's take a look at several teens who attempted suicide. They are very different sorts of people. Their problems aren't at all alike, yet somehow each came to the conclusion that "death" was the answer.

Ann

As a kid Ann had got along reasonably well with her parents. Now she couldn't communicate with them at all. When she looked in the mirror she saw a tall, clumsy-looking girl with oily hair and a bad complexion. She was fifteen, and it seemed to her that her breasts would never grow. When she complained, her parents told her she looked fine; she just had to be patient. Ann knew a cliché when she heard one, and she heard these over and over again. She couldn't seem to make them understand how unhappy she was.

Ann's parents thought she should study harder, but Ann hated school. Without friends she had to walk along the hall alone, and that was sheer torture. She had too much on her mind to worry about geometry and biology.

Besides, most of her classes were boring. Her teachers weren't particularly interested in reaching the students. They were only too happy to get out of the school building at the end of the day.

Then a miracle occurred. Ann fell in love with a boy in her Spanish class, and he asked her out. She was scared, but she had the courage to go out with him. When she found out he wanted to keep seeing her, it transformed her life.

Other boys began to notice her. She made friends with a couple of girls in the cafeteria at lunchtime. Most wonderful of all was really to be in love. Away from her boyfriend Ann felt miserable; with him she was overwhelmingly happy.

Then he broke off with her. It was the end of the world. Ann would break into tears just thinking about him. She had trouble sleeping. Her parents dismissed this as "adolescent moodiness," partly because they didn't want to see how deeply hurt she was, partly because teenagers do seem inexplicably moody to adults. The family doctor gave her some pills to help her sleep. Had Ann been over twenty, her parents would probably have taken her depression more seriously. They should have, anyway, because one day Ann took a whole bottle of sleeping pills. Her mother found her and Ann was rushed to the hospital. She was saved, but it was a close call.

Ann's parents were astounded by the suicide attempt. They had never imagined their daughter would try to kill herself. They had just assumed she would "get over this boy." But the loss of love, especially first love, can be devastating. Even popular teens have been shattered when it happens. Similarly, the death of a parent or divorce can make some teens exceedingly depressed. Loss and disruption are never trivial. Depression should never be treated lightly, and no suicide threat should ever be ignored. At the very least it's a cry for help.

Threatening to kill yourself, or even going so far as to try it, may be a way of signaling that you are desperate, not that you really want to die. It's a way of saying, "I don't know where to turn. I can't handle things alone anymore. Somebody, please rescue me."

Ken

Ken, seventeen, had made several suicide attempts. But his parents had always figured that they were "only" attempts and he wouldn't really do it. When he talked about suicide they dismissed it from their minds as "only" talk. These are common misconceptions about suicide, and some of the most dangerous. Unlike Ann, Ken wasn't one to hide in his room and cry. He took drugs and repeatedly ran away from home. He wasn't one of those quiet, withdrawn types who, according to popular legend, are suicide prone.

When Ken was sent to a military academy he hanged himself, leaving a note in which he claimed he was killing himself because his parents refused to buy him a new stereo. Ken had planned his death at an hour when he was expecting a visitor. A lot of suicides play this form of Russian roulette, and it is perhaps a sign that they don't really want to die. Unfortunately, the visitor didn't arrive and Ken died.

Sometimes when people feel very angry they not only strike out at others, they turn the anger inward upon themselves. Ken seemed to respond to pressure drastically. For him life was a combat zone. In a sense he became the victim of his own rage.

There are several theories about the suicide note he left. His latest fight with his parents had been over a stereo, so maybe the stereo was the last straw. Maybe it was a way of blaming his parents for his death; maybe he was incoherent and not thinking clearly by the time he wrote it. The note may seem crazy, but Ken, like most suicides, was not mentally ill. Again, this is another misconception.

Ethan

Ethan, sixteen, was good looking, a top student, an athlete, and had a lot of friends. He came from a wealthy family. Yet he shot himself after he flunked a chemistry test. Everyone was stunned. No one seemed more like a winner than Ethan.

One problem with understanding suicide is that we can only talk to the survivors, those who are rescued in time and those who change their mind or do not really want to die. There was nothing ambiguous about Ethan's attempt. He is dead. We can't ask him what went through his mind, how he felt, or any other questions we'd like answers to.

But we can take a closer look at Ethan's life and perhaps find some of the answers. Ethan was so successful, so good—perhaps a little too good. He had never learned to cope with pressure realistically. You can't be perfect. Everybody messes up sometimes, most of us a lot of the time. Ordinary living is stressful enough. If you always have to win, the stress is intolerable. If everything you try your hand at works, your first failure can be crippling. In this way Ethan's "success" was deceptive, because he had never learned to handle failure.

The tragedy of suicide is its finality. As people grow older, they tend to realize that death is the end—you cease to exist. Teens often don't believe that death is real. They often think that after they die they'll "magically" still be around, looking on.

But this isn't true. That's precisely why suicide is no solution. Nothing is solved for you when you die. You're just not here. Whether the people left behind will feel sorry about how they treated you won't matter to you anymore. You'll never know. Besides, they will go on living, and you will have denied yourself a lifetime. You will experience nothing further, good or bad. Nobody wins. You lose everything.

Ethan can't grow and change. Ken has no second chance. Had either of them lived, who knows? Perhaps Ethan would have learned to accept the fact that he was less than perfect, and still gone on to a successful life. Perhaps Ken would have broken away from his parents and been a lot happier at twenty than he was at fifteen.

So many people who attempt suicide in their teens never try it again. Take Ann: She's found a sympathetic therapist, is less depressed, and has even begun to go out with boys again. If you were to ask her today she'd tell you she's glad she didn't die, though at the time it seemed the only release from suffering. Also, she was drawn to the idea of suicide as a romantic gesture, something out of *Romeo and Juliet*. She would die for love.

Teenagers are sensitive, intense people with strong feelings. That makes them especially vulnerable to the mystique of suicide. They find it when they read novels. They see it when they go to the movies. There's the hero who throws his life away in battle for a worthy cause, the lovers who leap to their death rather than be separated, the lonely man or woman who swims out to sea in a beautiful sunset, never to be seen again.

Somehow, it never seems as if these suicides are really final. The hero's death is a triumph. The lovers are really together in some magic way after death. Who can believe that drowning would be painful and gruesome when the water is blue and the sunset so pretty? Actors who die on the screen can come back for another film. In real life that can't be done.

In the nineteenth century, the German writer Goethe wrote a highly romantic novel in which the young hero kills himself at the end. The publication of the novel was followed by a wave of suicides among young Germans. Actress Marilyn Monroe's suicide in 1962 also appears to have sparked an increase in suicides, particularly among the young, as did a suicide episode in a popular 1982 film, *An Officer and a Gentleman*.

John

John had a romantic notion of death. He also had a sneaking belief in his own immortality, and suicide held a morbid fascination for him. He knew that in Western religions suicide was considered a sin, and that to this day families of suicide victims often treat this form of dying as a shameful secret. All this only excited John's fascination with self-destruction. Being a teen he was something of a rebel, questioning ethical codes, defying the rules.

He was intrigued by the possibility of determining his own death, controlling when, where, and how it would happen. Of course, in his imagination he was present at his own funeral, watching everyone cry over him, regretting the way they'd treated him when he was alive. John found the idea of suicide so romantic that he wrote poems about it in a journal he kept. Killing himself, he thought, would be special, important, dramatic—a better fate than humdrum everyday living.

Lots of people have had John's fantasy. John turned it to reality and slashed his wrists. But dying was not what he'd expected. It wasn't clean or beautiful; it was violent, messy, and painful. He realized that death was oblivion, not sleep. He wouldn't be around to find out how anybody felt about him. It would literally be the end. He got to the phone and called for help. Luckily, the ambulance arrived in time. If it hadn't, his regrets wouldn't have made the least difference. It would have been the end.

Anyone You Know?

Perhaps you recognize yourself in one of these accounts. Maybe you've thought of other reasons for killing yourself. What can you do? If you feel as if you cannot stand to go on living, tell someone. You are not alone in what you feel, and part of you wants to live. Many others have been where you're at now, and they have survived.

If you have nowhere else to turn or are at a crisis point, call this toll-free number, 800-621-4000. This is a hot line where you can receive help for many problems, and where you can learn how to find someone to talk to near where you live. The front page of many metropolitan telephone directories lists the number of local crisis hot lines. And there is always the police emergency number. Remember, too, that at a moment of crisis you can always go to the emergency ward at your nearest hospital. Just walk in.

If it isn't you but a friend who's thinking of suicide, give them this information. Don't keep any friend's suicide threats a secret. Some secrets are fine, but not this one. You're not doing your friend any favor. This is one time you should approach an adult you trust, fast.

Depression

More stress than you can handle can make you very depressed without leading to attempts at suicide. There is a theory that people who take wild risks like driving eighty miles an hour, getting drunk all the time, taking heavy drugs, or starving themselves on a diet are really trying to kill themselves. On the other hand, maybe they're just trying to escape from pressure.

When you think of someone being depressed, you probably imagine them weighed down with problems, moving slowly, sleeping a lot, crying. But teenagers have a lot of energy. They can be wild and hyper when they're very depressed. The key is how you're feeling, not how you're acting.

When you're depressed, everything feels wrong. You're insecure, lacking in confidence. You see only the bleak, negative side of things. This sense that nothing good can ever happen to you again has a strange reality. The pessimistic view appears to be the only accurate and realistic one. Making things better in little ways doesn't seem to be worth the effort because you're certain you're doomed to fail.

Hitting a deep low once in a while is inevitable for almost everybody, adults included. It's only natural when at the very least you wake up to acne and oily hair, find yourself ignored by the top clique at school, get yelled at for handing in your homework late. Add to this a family crisis—your parents getting a divorce or your father losing his job—and there's no way to avoid a severe emotional down.

Depression often fades when a crisis eases. Sometimes it seems to vanish for no apparent reason. Maybe you've learned to handle stress better. Maybe you've learned to cope with a particular problem. Maybe there has been some internal chemical change that is as yet poorly understood by science. Whatever the reason, ups and downs are a normal part of living.

Pam It's another matter altogether when depression becomes deep or chronic. When it hangs around long after the reason for the depression has disappeared, then the depression itself becomes the problem. Pam wasn't particularly moody until she reached her senior year of high school. She had always done reasonably well in school, she got along okay with her friends, and she had no more than the usual run of problems with her parents.

The summer before her senior year Pam began to withdraw from her friends. She turned down boys who asked her out and said no when her friends asked her to go along to the movies. She said she liked being alone. She spent most of August watching television.

School started, but Pam didn't go out for girls' basketball, yearbook, or band, all activities she had been interested in before. She, who had always slept soundly and easily, had acute insomnia. She was only able to sleep two or three hours a night. Fatigue made it hard for her to concentrate and her marks dropped. That's when her parents began to worry. They called Pam's guidance counselor. He was someone Pam liked.

Pam went to see him, and as they talked, the reason for her depression became clear. Pam was afraid to go away to college. We live in a world that sets timetables for people, but we are not machines; we don't run like clockwork. At seventeen Pam wasn't ready to leave her home, her parents, her friends, and adapt simultaneously to the academic push of college.

Pam's family had always assumed she would go away to a top college. It took a little while for them to adjust to a different plan. In the end Pam opted to stay home and go to a community college nearby. She could have got a job or traveled for a year or so, but she wanted to stay in school. She came out of her depression by spring because she was no longer under excessive stress.

Josh Sometimes it's not that easy. At sixteen Josh had been through so much you could describe him as a burnout case. Stress had literally overwhelmed him. He was tired, he didn't enjoy anything, and he felt hopeless.

Josh's mother had abandoned him when he was a baby. He'd been through a series of foster homes. By thirteen he was on drugs. Now he was finished with drugs, but he was three years behind in school, had no family to help him, and didn't think that he could score high enough to get into the army.

That Josh should be seriously depressed makes perfect sense. It would be amazing if he weren't. There are limits to what any of us can be put through, how much stress we can take. There is nothing "crazy" about Josh's depression. He is reacting to a lifetime of being thwarted and defeated.

That doesn't mean it's hopeless for Josh, only that it will take more than his own internal resources to overcome depression. Maybe Josh will get into a special vocational program. Maybe he'll move and strike it lucky. Maybe he'll fall in love with a girl who can help him or find the right kind of surrogate family. Whatever happens, Josh has faced a lifetime of the kind of severe stress that takes a big toll.

If Josh's story reads like that of a battered fighter on the receiving end of a knock-out punch, and Pam sounds like a girl with a manageable problem, remember that both became very depressed. The causes of depression can also be murky and complex, as the following story shows.

Wendy   Wendy, like Pam, had never appeared to have any special difficulties getting along in the world. Then, at fifteen, she went on a diet. She had always been what her mother called "a picky eater." Now she ate next to nothing. She became obsessed with her appearance. No matter how thin she was, she always looked too fat when she gazed at herself in the mirror.

She lied to her parents about food, pretending to eat but throwing out food. She thought about food night and day, reading cookbooks for recreation and baking for others, but refusing to take a bite of food herself. She became compulsively neat—her room was as orderly as a monk's cell.

As if this weren't enough, Wendy took up exercise with a vengeance, jogging, swimming, pushing her body to the limits. Once in a while she'd go on a mad food binge, forcing herself to vomit afterward so that she wouldn't gain an ounce.

Wendy was five foot four. She went down to ninety pounds, eighty-six pounds, and at last seventy-nine pounds. She looked like a skeleton. Her parents, alarmed that she might literally starve herself to death or cause permanent damage to her body through malnourishment, had her hospitalized.

In the hospital she gained weight, and when released she began seeing a therapist. Wendy is a victim of anorexia nervosa, a condition that is becoming more common. It may take her years to recover. Meanwhile, she's isolated, unhappy, and still preoccupied with her weight.

There are many different ideas about what causes anorexia. Some people think it's a disease that afflicts mainly overly obedient, nonrebellious, teenage girls who are depressed and are trying to exert some control over their lives. This view is changing, as anorexia appears to be a far more widespread problem than anyone realized. Boys as well as girls can become anorectic, and no one personality type has a lock on the disease.

At the other end of the eating disorders scale, there are people who stuff themselves when they're miserable and become obese. Seriously depressed teens can become compulsive drinkers, drug addicts, runaways, or develop chronic headaches, stomachaches, and other physical symptoms.

It is a litany of terrors. Going over the list of awful things that can happen, you may wonder how you're going to make it at all. Often it isn't easy, but practically everyone does make it.

Remember that marvelous store of adaptation energy that nature has provided. Teens have an amazing ability to bounce back from even the lowest of lows. And bounce back quickly, but not immediately. Sometimes you may need outside help, a psychologist, or a doctor. Sometimes a living situation may be so stressful that some sort of change is required. Often what you need most is time.

It would be nice if we could explain how the passage of

time can banish suicidal thoughts or lift a deep depression. Some day, medical science may be able to understand the exact biological mechanism that governs moods and feelings, so that they can be charted and treated when they become serious, with the same efficiency with which science treats infectious diseases. Some day—but not yet. At the moment there are plenty of theories, but very little is certain.

The only thing we can be absolutely certain about is time—it works. Give yourself plenty of time, time for that marvelous stock of adaptation energy you possess to build up once again and allow you to cope effectively with the world.

10

Stress and Tension

YOU FIND YOURSELF IN A HIGHLY STRESSFUL SITUATION. Let's say that you are at a party where you know hardly anyone. You stand in a corner hoping that someone will come over and talk to you. But no one does. People pass you by without noticing. Or they seem to be giving you funny looks.

You can feel the muscles tightening in the back of your neck. A dull ache creeps down your arms, and your stomach begins to act as if it's tied up in knots.

That's all muscle tension—one of the most common reactions to stress, and one that is misunderstood and whose importance is underestimated. It is underestimated because not only is muscle tension a reaction to stress but it also helps to *increase* stress—the tension itself becomes a source of stress.

You may think tension is a minor, stress-related problem, something that goes away after the stressful situation
is over. Wrong. Muscle tension is insidious. In the example
of the party, you are fully aware of the tension. But you
are probably walking around right now with a lot of muscle tension that you don't feel. The body seems able to
adjust to higher and higher levels of tension. That doesn't
mean that the tension is good for you, or even that it is
harmless. It just means that you are not consciously aware
of the tension. In this case, what you don't know *can* hurt
you.

There are two types of muscles in the human body—
voluntary and involuntary. The voluntary muscles are
those that move our arms, legs, eyebrows, and so forth.
The involuntary muscles are those of the interior organs,
such as the heart, and those that control the action of the
colon, or of the uterus during labor.

The term *voluntary muscles* is something of a misnomer.
Though we can generally control the movements of these
muscles, often they move without our conscious control.
When we hear a loud noise we may "jump" or "start." The
voluntary muscles have moved automatically, without conscious control. When we get very nervous the muscles of
our throat may tighten up so that we can barely talk.
Again, this is a situation in which normally voluntary muscles react without conscious control. In some cases we can
develop a twitch or tic, an obviously involuntary motion of
a set of voluntary muscles.

The involuntary muscles normally move smoothly and
rhythmically. They are generally thought to be beyond
conscious or emotional control. But the smooth functioning of these muscles can be upset by the emotions. That's
why some athletes are sick to their stomachs before the big
game, and it's why you get a knot in your stomach when

you get stuck in a corner at a party. It's also why your heart seems to speed up, pound, or even skip a beat under stressful conditions.

The Freeze Reaction

Why do muscles so often tense up when we are under stress? It all seems to go back to the old fight or flight reaction. The muscles contract in preparation to fight or run. There may also be a third part to the fight or flight reaction that contributes to muscular tension. It is the "freeze" reaction. When threatened, many animals will simply freeze—stand still without moving a muscle. It's a protective reaction, since a nonmoving object is less likely to be seen by an enemy. It is quite possible that our ancestors habitually froze when threatened with danger, and freeze has become, like fight or flight, part of our evolutionary heritage. Of course, when you or any other animal freezes, all of the muscles are under great tension. They must contract and stay contracted so that nothing moves. Make your arm go rigid, and hold it that way. You will find that the muscles are tense and that it takes energy just to hold the arm rigid. Hold it long enough and it will become painful.

As we have said before, many of these reactions are no longer of much use in modern society. Indeed, they may be harmful, but we are stuck with them. When we are faced with a situation—like a party which is socially stressful—we still tend to react much the same way our ancestors did when faced with a hungry saber-toothed tiger. We tense up, ready for some sort of action. Today, no action is required, and freezing in a corner so no one notices you isn't much help either. So we just become tense for no good purpose, and often we stay that way for a long time.

Sometimes we are aware of what is happening. The muscles tense up to such a degree that they actually become painful. Sometimes we are aware of the tension only when it's over. When we have survived a stressful situation we are overwhelmed with a feeling of blessed relief and muscular relaxation—even though we were not entirely aware of the muscular tension during the situation.

And that brings us to the significant point. While the mind is very efficient at generating muscular tension, it is not very good at recognizing the tension, and it isn't very good at relaxing. Medical researchers using sensitive instruments that measure muscular tension have been able to measure high levels of tension in people who thought that their muscles were perfectly relaxed. The tension was there; the people just didn't know it.

Muscles can do only two things, contract and relax. A muscle or group of muscles will contract in response to some sort of stimulus. When the stimulus is withdrawn the muscles relax, but they do not relax quickly, and they do not necessarily relax completely. Even in sleep, when you would think that the muscles are completely relaxed, there can be a great deal of tension. Anyone who has awakened in the morning, jaw aching from a night of teeth clenching, knows this.

Since the tension diminishes slowly, the muscles can still be at a high level of tension when a new tension-producing situation occurs or if one keeps mentally recreating the original situation. Muscle tension is thus sustained at higher and higher levels as time goes on.

Consciously, we may not be aware of the increase in tension in ourselves, though we can see it clearly in others. People who have a lot of tension are often, and very appropriately, referred to as being "uptight." And as Dr. Barbara Brown, one of the pioneers in the study of stress and muscle tension, notes, "Uptight people usually startle easily and vigorously." An active startle reaction is fine for a rabbit on the lookout for a fox. It's not necessary if you're just sitting in your room and jump a mile every time the phone rings.

Patterns of Tension

Our muscular tension tends to fall into certain patterns. Here is how that works. Let us imagine you have gotten very angry at someone, and unconsciously you clench your fists. It's preparation for hitting the person. But you never strike the blow. And you may not even know that you have clenched your fists.

You may continue to clench your fists every time you meet that person or even think about him. And that may go on long after your original anger has cooled. Once the pattern is established, you may clench your fists every time you get angry at anyone or anything. Those muscles may never really relax, and that will create a lot of muscle tension.

A constant, high level of muscular tension created by stress can lead to a large number of unpleasant physical conditions. There is, for example, the tension headache, one of the most common forms of headache. Sometimes stressful situations can trigger tension headaches, which may range from mild to blindingly severe. There are individuals who simply cannot function when in the grip of a tension headache because they are in so much pain. It feels as if there is something severely wrong inside the head.

But sensitive muscle-monitoring devices have shown that the source of the pain in the tension headache is extremely tight muscles in the forehead, scalp, and back of the neck. If you have a tension headache it isn't really inside your head; it's in muscles you probably didn't even know you had.

Keeping the muscles tense and contracted drains energy, so muscular tension leads to a feeling of fatigue. It can also keep you from sleeping properly. Muscular tension is one of the chief causes of insomnia. It's hard to face the stress of the day when you are absolutely beat. So stress-created tension is not just a minor problem, and it leads to a whole range of additional problems.

Perhaps the most insidious feature of tension is that besides being created by mental stress, once a pattern of tension is established it tends to reinforce the mental stress, indeed even to create it. Let's go back to our opening example of the party. Now let's say you don't take easily to new social situations—most people don't. As soon as you enter an unfamiliar group your muscles tense up, and your mind is assailed by feelings of great anxiety.

While the process originally started in your mind and was communicated to your muscles, the muscular tension begins to take on an existence of its own. Now the muscular tension that you feel—and often tension that you do not feel—when you enter an unfamiliar social situation feeds back to the mind and increases the mental anguish, which in turn increases the tension of the muscles, in a never-ending vicious cycle. Your mind tells your muscles something is wrong, so they tense up, and your muscles tell your mind they are tense, so something must be wrong. As a result you feel absolutely rotten at parties.

You can tell yourself mentally to relax, to stop being so anxious, because nothing terrible is going to happen. But as you probably already know, that sort of personal pep talk doesn't work very well. One of the best ways of coping with many stressful situations is by working backward, and reducing the muscular tension first. Once the muscular tension is reduced the mental anguish often tends to subside.

Train to Relax

Of course you can't just say to your muscles, "Okay, you're voluntary muscles. I'm the boss, and I command you to relax so I can feel better." That won't work. In the first place you are probably not even aware which muscles are tense, and since you did not consciously cause them to tense up, you cannot consciously compel them to relax. But your muscles can be trained to relax. There are a number of excellent and very practical techniques for doing this.

The first essential step in reducing the tension caused by stress is simply to be aware of the fact that the tension exists. Find out what tension feels like.

Here is the traditional demonstration of muscular tension: Raise one arm so that the palm of the hand is facing outward away from your face. Now bend the wrist backward, and try to point the fingers back toward your forearm. That will produce a feeling of strain on the wrist joint. But the muscles of the back of the hand and the wrist have been contracted, and so you should feel the muscle tension as well. Now flop your hand forward with the fingers pointing downward. Don't push it; just let it drop. That is the tension-relaxation cycle.

This demonstration was first used in 1908 by Edmund

Jacobson, who developed a popular technique called progressive relaxation. It was Jacobson's theory that mental anxiety and muscular tension were intimately related, and that if your muscles were really relaxed you would not, indeed could not, feel anxious.

Jacobson's experiments led him to believe that as we mentally review our problems, our muscles tense up in various ways. Even when we are not aware of it, we are bracing for a blow. He went on to conclude that if mental images can produce the tension, then mental images can also be used to reduce it. Further, once the muscular tension is reduced, then the mental anxiety also goes down.

Jacobson's theories are, to say the very least, controversial in the medical world. Very few medical scientists believe that all mental problems can be treated by simply relaxing the muscles. But Jacobson's technique, progressive relaxation, works. It has been widely used to reduce both muscular tension and mental anxiety. The technique doesn't solve all the stress-related problems Jacobson thought it would. Like so many other popular theories on how to feel better, too much was claimed for it. But progressive relaxation therapy is often recommended by doctors who don't necessarily believe in the whole theory behind it. Even if it is not perfect, it is often effective. And it might be effective for you.

The first thing one must learn about relaxation is that it does not come automatically. You have to work at being relaxed. It takes time, and the more time you spend, the better you will become at relaxing. There are a number of variations of the progressive relaxation technique, and they have been promoted under a variety of labels. The basic principles are all the same. There are no hidden or magic secrets.

You must set aside a period of time, ten or fifteen minutes every day, to practice relaxation. You need a quiet place where you are not likely to be disturbed. You don't have to find a cave or hide in the attic. Your room would be fine. Just close the door and take the phone off the hook. And pick a time of day when you are less likely to be disturbed by someone knocking at your door. Make yourself comfortable. Sit in a comfortable chair, lie on your bed, or on the floor if you like. It doesn't matter, just so long as you are comfortable.

When you begin to use progressive relaxation the first thing you must do is learn what relaxation feels like. As we have already pointed out, you are often unaware of tension in your muscles; in fact, as we said earlier, you probably have muscles that you don't even know about. And these may be the source of great tension. So you start tensing and relaxing little groups of muscles, basically just to see what relaxation feels like and to become aware of all the muscles you have. You can start with the muscles of your head, or the muscles of your feet—it doesn't make any difference. Let's say you start at the head.

1. Raise your eyebrows by opening your eyes as wide as possible.

2. Tense the muscles on either side of your nose as if you were going to sneeze.

3. Flare out your nostrils.

4. Make a big grin while clenching your teeth.

5. Draw up first one corner of your mouth, then the other.

6. Pull your chin down as close to your chest as possible.

7. Draw your head back as far as possible.

If you want to start at the other end, you can curl and uncurl your toes. Then you can hold out one leg and point the toes as far forward as possible and then as far backward. Turn your foot outward as far as you can, and then turn it inward as far as you can.

Go through your entire body this way. Clench your fists. Roll your wrists around. Move your shoulder blades back and forth. Suck in your stomach; then push it out. Do the same with your chest. In short, try to tense up and then release every voluntary muscle in your body. Don't tense them all at once. Start at one end and work your way up, or down. After you do this for a while you will become more aware of the muscles in your body, and what relaxation of these muscles feels like.

Images of Relaxation

Awareness of your muscles is one part of relaxation. Imagery is the other. Since the mind helps to create muscular tension, it can also help relax that tension. So when you are practicing relaxation, you have to put yourself in the proper frame of mind. Try to imagine yourself in some relaxing setting—sitting by the ocean or in front of an open fire, floating in a tub of warm water, or whatever. Try to exclude all troubling thoughts from your mind. That's easier said than done, we know. If you are already in an extremely agitated state, it is probably best not to try to start relaxation training. You may be too upset and excited, and give up before you have really been properly launched into the technique. Start learning to relax when you're reasonably calm. Then, after you have practiced for

a while you will be able to use the technique even when you
are upset, because you will have mastered it.

In order to relax you must mentally give yourself in-
structions. Here is the technique as described by Dr.
Eugene Walker in his book *Learn to Relax:*

*I am going to relax completely. First, I will relax my forehead
and scalp. I will let all the muscles of my forehead and scalp relax
and become completely at rest. All the wrinkles will come out of my
forehead and that part of my body will relax completely. Now I will
relax the muscles of my face. I will just let them relax and go limp.
There will be no tension in my jaw. Next, I will relax my neck
muscles. Just let them become tranquil and allow all the pressure to
leave them. My neck muscles are relaxing completely. Now, I will
relax the muscles of my shoulders. That relaxation will spread
down my arms to the elbows, down the forearms to the wrists,
hands and fingers. My arms will just dangle from the frame of m*
*body. I will now relax the muscles of my chest. I will let them relax.
I will take a deep breath and relax, letting all the tightness and
tenseness leave. My breathing will now be normal and relaxed,
and I will relax the muscles of my stomach. Now I will relax all the
muscles up and down both sides of the spine; now the waist,
buttocks and thighs down to my knees. Now the relaxation will
spread to the calves of my legs, ankles, feet and toes. I will just lie
here and continue to let all of the muscles go completely limp. I will
become completely relaxed from the top of my head to the tips of my
toes.*

It may sound a bit silly, but it really will work.

Regular daily relaxation can help to reduce the tensions
brought on by normal daily stress. It can also be used in
special situations. When facing an unusually stressful time,
a ten- or fifteen-minute session of relaxation can do won-

ders, if you can find the time and a quiet place to lie down.

Those who are really proficient at this technique can use it even more frequently, and with little special preparation. For example, when facing a difficult test they can find a corner, sit down, and in a few moments become fully relaxed and refreshed.

But as we said, this is not a technique that comes automatically; it must be learned and practiced. And, as with all physical activities, there are some people who are better at it than others. Relaxation will not cure all your problems, but almost everybody can benefit to some degree.

Progressive relaxation is an old technique. It has many imitators that have been presented under a variety of names. It doesn't make any difference what the technique is called. If properly practiced, most of these techniques will work to produce muscle relaxation.

Yoga

This is an ancient technique. Yoga is a complex system of mind and body control that has developed over the centuries in India. Very simple forms of yoga have become popular in the West. Here, yoga is used as an exercise and as a means of relieving muscular tension caused by stress. Yoga classes are offered in many schools, Ys, and community centers. The exercises seem a little exotic at first, but there is really nothing bizarre or magical about them. Yoga can be an effective stress and tension reliever.

Biofeedback

For some, the muscular tension produced by stressful situations can be debilitating. It can, for example, produce blinding tension headaches. For such individuals simple relaxation procedures may not be enough. Tension headaches have been treated with all manner of therapies and drugs, but one of the most successful treatments is called biofeedback training.

As we said, people often have extreme muscular tension without being consciously aware of it. The biofeedback procedure uses electronic sensors which give off a tone when muscles are tense. The tone decreases in volume as the tension decreases. That is biofeedback; the patient is being fed back information about his or her biological condition. Thus, people know instantly when they are relaxing, and this makes relaxation easier. Without the sensors, they might not be able to tell that there was tension in the first place or that relaxation was taking place. The theory behind all biofeedback is that the more you know about your body the better you will be able to control it.

Early experimental success with biofeedback training led to an outburst of enthusiastic publicity about the technique. It was hailed as a potential cure for all manner of stress and tension-related ailments from tooth grinding to high blood pressure. It was looked upon as a way to relieve anxiety, insomnia, alcoholism, and drug abuse. It was to allow patients to take control of their own treatment. It was a beautiful dream.

Unfortunately, as with many new treatments, the initial

enthusiasm was followed by a string of disappointments. Biofeedback was not a cure-all. The problems of stress-related conditions like anxiety and high blood pressure were more complicated and difficult to treat than the early biofeedback enthusiasts had believed. Biofeedback publicity waned, and public interest dropped.

Still, the field of biofeedback remains a promising one. It holds out the possibility that with further research we will be able to get a better hold on the many stress-related conditions that afflict us, and that we will be able to exercise greater conscious control over our bodies. Once we do this we can reduce dependence on drugs or other potentially harmful treatments. There are some hospitals and clinics that offer biofeedback training for such conditions as tension headaches.

A Few Easy Exercises

For most of us biofeedback training is still a distant promise. And perhaps learning some form of the progressive relaxation technique is more than you can do at the moment. There are still a few simple exercises and techniques based on the relaxation theory, that you can use to relieve some common, stress-caused tensions. They will make you feel better.

One of the most common reactions to stressful situations is setting the jaw and clenching the teeth. The result can be tense and painful muscles of the jaw and neck. To relieve this extremely common stress-caused condition, Dr. Charles F. Strobel recommends this simple exercise. Let your jaw hang open and gently move it back and forth with your fingers until you find the position which is most comfortable; then gently massage the jaw. Close your eyes, relax, and hold the position for about a minute.

Another common site of tension is the muscles of the neck and shoulders. After a stressful day these muscles can feel tight, even painful. To relieve the tension, tilt your head forward, try to touch your chest. Hold that position for fifteen seconds. Then tilt the head back as far as you can for another fifteen seconds. Repeat to the right and left sides—fifteen seconds each. Then slowly rotate your head in a circle, first one way and then the other.

Sometimes tension in the muscles of the feet can cause them to ache painfully and generally increase your feeling of fatigue as well. Try this: Lie on your back and put your feet up. Now circle one foot ten times, flex and straighten it ten times, and repeat the action with the other foot.

One of the most frightening, or at least embarrassing, stress-caused conditions is a "panic attack." You face an extremely stressful situation and suddenly your body feels completely out of control; you begin taking quick short breaths, as though you had just run a race. The condition is common, and temporary. What you must do is find a quiet place to sit down and try to relax. Take long deep, slow breaths. Count to three as you breathe in through your nose. Then breathe out through your mouth while you count four and five. Not only will your breathing become more regular, but the feeling of panic will also begin to subside, and you will be able to take a more measured and rational look at the situation that triggered the attack.

None of these little exercises is a cure-all for the tension caused by stress. But since stress is an inevitable part of your life, such exercises help you cope more effectively. They help you take control of the tension rather than allowing the tension to take control of you.

Athletics and Exercise

Athletics and exercise have always been regarded as great relievers of muscular tension and wonderful antidotes to stress. And so they are. Practically any form of exercise does tend to loosen muscles that may be tense and tight.

While we recognize that exercise itself is a stressor, it can be a highly beneficial one. Remember that we discussed specific stress and how useful it is to divert stress from one area to another. Most of the severe negative stress—the distress—that we suffer from in the modern world is mental and emotional. So putting some stress on the body can be a wonderful way of getting away from the stress generated by the mind and the emotions.

In highly stressful situations you may find you feel a bit better if you can pace up and down. Sometimes you just can't help it, because you can't sit still. A long walk might be better than pacing, and a long run better still.

A regular exercise program is good for your physical health and can be very good for your mental health. These facts have been recognized for a long time. The virtues of exercise have been widely praised.

But wait, doctors have begun to recognize something else about athletics and exercise. They have begun to recognize there can be too much of a good thing. In America today some people, particularly young people, have been reaching that stage.

In February 1983, Catherine Shisslak of the Arizona Health Sciences Program of the University of Arizona and two of her colleagues, Dr. Alayne Yates and Dr. Kevin

Leehy, wrote an article for the *New England Journal of Medicine* that said what a lot of doctors had come to feel—that there are a significant number of people today who are simply exercising too hard. They have become "compulsive athletes," and this has grown into a serious national health problem, most acute among the young. The article went on to say that many of the compulsive athletes have personalities similar to those of individuals suffering from anorexia nervosa. Indeed, many anorectics were either deeply involved in athletics or could trace the origin of their disorder to an athletically inspired weight-control program.

The problem of compulsive athletes has grown enormously over the past ten years, and it is believed that the majority of victims are young women. This may be because the emphasis on women's athletics has changed so much over this period. At one time any form of hard competitive athletics seemed out of the question for most women. People doubted a woman could run a mile, much less a marathon. That's all changed now, and changed for the better. But the change has also created problems. Exercise is a stressor, and it can be a particularly potent stressor when combined with the pressures of athletic competition. For women athletes, and men as well, you can't just say that the more exercise they take, the better. With exercise, as with every other stress-producing activity, there is a breaking point.

In March 1983 the *New York Times* told the tragic story of seventeen-year-old Mary Wazeter, a promising distance runner whose obsessive devotion to her sport had driven her into anorexia and finally to a suicide attempt that had left her paralyzed from the chest down.

The case of Mary Wazeter is an extreme one. And the specter of becoming a "compulsive athlete" shouldn't scare anyone off exercise, or from serious involvement in competitive athletics. But you must remind yourself that all of that exercising, all of that conditioning, does create stress. The stress can be bearable, even beneficial, but there is also a point where the body becomes exhausted. We're not talking of the temporary exhaustion that is caused by a day of hard training; that's normal. We're talking about long-term exhaustion, the kind you don't snap back from after a good night's rest. You have to be able to step back from your athletic activity and ask yourself if you still really enjoy what you are doing. If you don't, and your only goal seems to be to push yourself farther and harder, then you may be getting too much of a good thing, and it's time to ease off.

11

Unstressing the Mind

THE MODERN AGE IS A STRESSFUL ONE; NO ONE CAN DENY that. We may very well be living through one of the most stressful periods in human history. There is rapid technological change, and the structure of the family is under pressure—for example, your values may be very different from those of your parents. And above it all hangs the threat of nuclear annihilation. No wonder you're anxious. No wonder you feel under great stress.

But are we really under that much more stress than people of past ages? It's hard to say. For most people, life has never been easy and tranquil. There have been many periods of change—the industrial revolution, for example, the religious upheavals of the Reformation, or the periods when the plague killed millions of people.

Certainly the teenage years have always been difficult.

Here is what Shakespeare had to say about them in *The Winter's Tale:* "I wish there were no age between ten and three-and-twenty, or that youth would sleep out the rest; for there is nothing in the between but getting wenches with child, wronging the ancientry, stealing, fighting."

The threat of the plague was no less real than the threat of the bomb, and in many societies there has been an endless struggle just to find enough to eat.

Perhaps we are exposed to more stressors today than were people of past ages, particularly mental stressors. However, while this observation is widely repeated, there is no way of proving it. There is no remotely accurate way of determining whether we have more stress-related problems than people did in the past. Throughout history people have complained that the age they lived in was not as happy as ages past. Since people have always faced some degree of stress they must have had ways of coping with it. Are there basic biological ways of coping with stress that we have somehow forgotten?

Dr. Herbert Benson of the Harvard Medical School believes that just as we have a fight or flight response, we also have a relaxation reponse. His research indicates that certain conditions trigger automatic relaxation reactions in the body, in which the blood pressure is lowered, breathing becomes deeper and more even, the heart rate slows, there is a general relaxation of muscle tension, and the level of certain hormones in the blood tends to decrease. There is even a change in brain wave patterns as the mind enters a more tranquil state. All physical measurements indicate a lowering of the body's stress level. This condition is what Dr. Benson has called the *relaxation response.* In many respects it is the exact opposite of the fight or flight response. Like that fight or flight response, it is natural and automatic, but unfortunately it isn't triggered nearly as often as it should be. While our fight or flight button is pushed all the time, the relaxation response is hardly triggered at all in modern society.

Dr. Benson arrived at his relaxation response theories by a rather unusual route. He had been studying the technique of Transcendental Meditation, popularly called TM, which had become quite fashionable, even faddish, in the United States during the 1970s. The technique had been brought to the United States from India by the Maharishi Mahesh Yogi. At its core the practice of TM is very simple. It consists of sitting quietly for two fifteen- or twenty-minute periods a day and silently repeating a secret word or "mantra" to oneself. This was supposed to produce a profoundly peaceful state and was generally promoted as an antidote to the stresses of modern life.

The Maharishi's technique was surrounded with a good deal of Hindu ceremonial and secrecy, hardly surprising since that is the religion from which TM was adapted. The TM movement also began to make much grander claims about providing "perfect bliss" and solving all the world's as well as all personal problems. After a while TM changed from being a widespread popular movement to a small cult, which made increasingly bizarre claims. But we must not let the cultish aspects of TM obscure the real reason for its popularity. It was and is an effective method of lowering stress.

Scientific Proof A lot of TM's initial popularity was sparked by the results of a scientific study of meditators conducted by, among others, Dr. Herbert Benson. The doctors monitored blood pressure, respiration rate and perspiration, muscle tension, blood chemistry, and even the brain waves of the meditators.

In the widely publicized study, the researchers announced that, somewhat to their surprise, they found that meditation did what it was advertised to do. It put subjects into a state of profound relaxation.

The measurements taken from the meditators were compared to measurements taken from a control group of subjects who were simply sitting quietly. Both meditators and nonmeditators looked as if they were doing the same thing, sitting quietly, but the instruments showed their bodily reactions were very different.

The meditators showed dramatic increases of skin resistance (a measure of relaxation), decreases in the level of blood lactate, oxygen consumption, and respiration, and a host of other physiological changes which indicated that the meditators were in a state of profound rest—a "general quiescence of the nervous system," said the researchers' report. They were even more relaxed than they would have been if they had been sleeping.

The degree of relaxation attained by the meditators is even more remarkable when you realize that throughout the meditation they were in laboratory settings and were hooked up to a host of measuring devices. There were electrodes stuck to their heads to measure brain waves, sensors wrapped around their chests to measure respiration, and catheters stuck in their arms to chart changes in blood chemistry. It's hard to imagine anyone relaxing under such conditions, but the meditators were able to do it with ease.

The research report concluded that TM produced a distinctly different state of consciousness and that the procedure "may have practical applications." The most obvious practical application was that TM might be used to alleviate excessive stress by promoting relaxation.

While TM worked, there was nothing magical or particularly original about it. TM simply employed techniques that have been used, with slight variations, in many societies. Usually these techniques were used in a religious context, but not always.

In the Middle Ages meditation had been widely used in Christian countries. Christian meditators didn't use a secret Sanskrit word or mantra to repeat silently to themselves—they used a simple word like God or love. Zen Buddhists didn't use any word at all; they just concentrated on their breathing. And the nineteenth-century English poet Alfred, Lord Tennyson was able to put himself into a meditative state by sitting quietly and repeating his own name silently to himself.

People living in traditional societies, such as the Australian aborigines, will often withdraw to a quiet spot and sit in a state of silent reverie which could be called meditation. Researchers have noted that apes and monkeys will often be found sitting quietly, with their eyes closed, but not sleeping. Who is to say that they are not meditating, or doing something very much like meditating?

Four Basic Elements

The profound state of relaxation evoked by meditation is the result of what researchers call the relaxation response. Four basic elements are needed for triggering this response. They are:

1. *A quiet environment.* Historically, people have meditated in churches and temples. Such places are usually islands of calm in a world which can often be hectic and noisy. It is not necessary that the place chosen for meditation be holy. It is only important that it not be noisy.

2. *A mental device.* In TM it was the secret mantra, but

any device that focuses attention will do as well. It can consist of repeating any simple word, concentrating on breathing, or gazing at an object—either a religious object such as a cross or a nonreligious object such as a candle flame or a swinging pendulum. The important thing is to have something that will keep the meditator's mind from wandering off and concentrating on troubling or exciting thoughts which disrupt the relaxation.

3. *A passive attitude.* This is the hardest part, because no type of meditation can be pushed. If distracting thoughts pop up, the meditator is advised not to worry about them or pursue them, but just bring the mind back to the mantra or other device. Meditators are also taught not to worry about how they are doing, but adopt a "let it happen" attitude and return to concentration on the mental device. For those of us used to constant activity, the passive attitude is hard to achieve.

4. *A comfortable position.* People often think of meditators having to assume some sort of special position, either the cross-legged lotus position or kneeling. This is not necessary; it is only necessary that the meditator be comfortable—but not too comfortable—because the meditator is not supposed to fall asleep. Meditating is not sleeping, and if you lie down on a comfortable bed you will probably fall asleep. The lotus position and some of the other relatively difficult postures assumed by meditators in some societies may have evolved as ways to keep them from falling asleep. As with the mantra, there is nothing magical about the position.

After identifying the four basic elements necessary for evoking the relaxation response, Dr. Benson developed his own system of meditation which he tested on subjects at a Boston hospital. He found that his system worked as well as TM or any other system.

The Benson system is really an adaptation of TM, which in itself was an adaptation of earlier Indian techniques. What Benson did was remove the variety of religious and mystical elements which surrounded it. He felt that a non-religious, nonmystical technique would be more acceptable to most people in the West today. It was also easier to learn. You didn't need a guru or teacher. It could be learned from a book. But Dr. Benson also stressed that any meditative technique, so long as it contained the four basic elements, would work equally well, if you stick to it.

The Modern Technique

1. Find a quiet place where you are not likely to be disturbed for twenty minutes or so. Absolute quiet is not necessary, but a room with a loud radio playing or a place where someone is likely to come up and talk to you is not acceptable.

2. Sit down in a comfortable position and close your eyes.

3. Relax, or relax as far as you are able. At first you might wish to use a little of the progressive relaxation technique by relaxing the muscles of your feet first, then moving upward. Complete relaxation, however, is not necessary, and once you have been meditating regularly the relaxation should become automatic.

4. Breathe through your nose, easily and naturally. Every time you breathe out silently repeat the word "one." That is your mental device, your mantra. Breathe in, breathe out "one," breathe in, breathe out "one."

5. Do this for ten to twenty minutes twice a day, if possible. Don't worry too much about how much time you

spend meditating. A few minutes more or less won't make any difference. You can open your eyes and check your watch or look at the clock. Do not set an alarm, because you would worry about when it was going to go off, and the noise would startle you. Spend about as much time as you feel comfortable with, then stop. After the meditation period is over, don't jump up. Sit with your eyes closed for a few minutes. As you become more practiced, you may be able to sit with your eyes open.

6. While you are sitting repeating "one," don't worry if you don't suddenly feel completely relaxed. Don't worry if you feel fidgety. You are not trying to get anywhere. Just let things happen. If distracting thoughts occur, simply try to ignore them, let them go, and go back to repeating "one." But don't worry if you do get distracting thoughts.

For a while you will not feel as if you are achieving anything. Don't worry about that either. With practice you will get better at the technique and relaxation will occur automatically. Remember that the relaxation response is an automatic biological response. All you have to do is set up the right conditions for triggering it.

There are two notes of caution. First, you are advised not to try this system or any other meditative technique for two hours after eating. It seems that the digestive process somehow interferes with the relaxation response. And, of course, drugs or alcohol are absolutely forbidden.

Second, it is best not to start training in the technique when you are extremely anxious or under an unusual amount of stress. You might say, but that's when I really need to relax. True enough, and the technique should help you later. But when you are just learning, simply sitting quietly may actually make things worse, because the mind will be opened up to all sorts of awful thoughts. A simple mental device will not be strong enough to banish them. After you have learned the technique, it may serve very well in exceptionally stressful periods. But when first starting out, if you find yourself feeling more, rather than less anxious, stop. This may not be the moment for you to start learning meditation.

Meditation isn't going to solve all your stress-related problems. If you approach the practice with modest expectations—that here is a technique that will help you cope more effectively with the normal stresses of daily life—then you might find it very useful indeed. But as with progressive relaxation, and practically everything else in life, it isn't an instant cure. You have to practice it.

Stress Inoculation

There is another mental technique that can help you deal with stress, particularly specific stressful situations, like a big test or an important interview.

The technique is called stress inoculation. One of the greatest advances in the history of medicine was the discovery of inoculation. If a person was injected with a minute quantity of bacteria this would build up the body's defenses and thus prevent a serious attack of that disease at a later date.

You can inoculate yourself against some of the harmful effects of stress, but you don't get an injection, you have to do it mentally. Says Dr. Dennis Turk, assistant professor of psychology at Yale University, "Gradually exposing yourself to a small amount of stress before you enter a high pressure situation can actually boost your emotional defenses against it."

Stress inoculation is particularly useful for teens who

often find themselves thrown into situations without adequate knowledge or protection.

The key to stress inoculation is to plan ahead mentally. Try to imagine what's going to happen and how you will react to it. Think the situation through step by step. "By chunking a big problem into manageable proportions you figure out how you'll survive," says Dr. Donald Meichenbaum, professor of psychiatry at Waterloo University in Ontario, Canada. "Then whatever happens when you're in the situation, you know how to try managing that problem and what you'll do next."

The imagination has to be disciplined, however. Because without discipline imagination can run wild and create panic. "Once you know exactly what will happen you can respond to realities, not imagined catastrophes," Dr. Meichenbaum says. It is the imagined catastrophes that panic us most often.

Let's say you're facing a tough exam. You've done all the studying you can, and you feel reasonably well prepared. But you're also scared. You think that you're going to go into the exam and panic, and forget what you've taken so much time and trouble to learn.

Try to figure out exactly what it is that usually sets off panic. Is it your first look at the exam questions? At that moment your mind seems to suddenly go blank. You feel you'll never remember a thing.

If that is the sort of thing that happens to you, or if you fear it will happen to you, just recognize that you are going to have that blank moment. Then figure out the best way to react. Is it to sit quietly for a moment, regain your composure, and absorb the questions? Perhaps it is best to go on to the next question or read the entire test through and find the easiest parts. Have a plan. Know what you're going to do. Be ready for the stress.

Or let's say you tend to panic about halfway through a test. You see someone else finishing up when you feel you have barely begun. Why are you being so slow? You'll never finish on time! Panic! Perhaps you have finished an essay and you see others writing away. More panic! What do they know that you don't? You try to think of more to say, but can't. Once again, you must think the situation through carefully. Plan your reactions. Be mentally prepared for finishing last, or first, or anywhere in between.

The stressful situation may be a personal one—breaking up with a boyfriend or girlfriend. Again, think about how you are going to do it. When am I going to tell the other person? How will the other person react? How will I feel? Try to be as realistic as possible with yourself. Then act according to plan.

One of the best things that you can do is to remind yourself that no matter what situation you face, it isn't the end of the world for you. It may feel like it, but it isn't. Be prepared for that end-of-the-world feeling too.

If you blow the test, you blow it. Not nice to be sure, but you will survive. After a breakup you don't have to conclude that you'll never love anybody again. There will be others. It is often very helpful to talk to people who have already been through a similar situation.

Sometimes the best thing you can do when facing a difficult problem, says Dr. Meichenbaum, is not to think about it, at least for a while. Say you see your ex-boyfriend or girlfriend with someone else. There's nothing you can do about it—so try to tune it out for a while. At another time you may be able to handle thinking about that situation a bit more calmly.

Many of life's problems just go away after a little while. Or your feelings about the problem change so much that it doesn't seem to be much of a problem anymore. You don't have to rush around and try to find a solution to every problem. Procrastination and avoidance are not always wrong. There are plenty of times when they can be the best thing for you.

Each time that you cope successfully with a stressful situation, or you manage to successfully avoid one, you will become stronger. You will develop skills that will help you cope with a similar situation the next time you confront it. One of the toughest things about being young is that you have to meet a lot of situations for the first time. Without experience behind you, many situations are extremely stressful. As you gain experience they become less stressful. You learn what works best, and you learn that even if things don't go well you do survive.

But before you gain that sort of experience you can inoculate yourself against stress by mentally rehearsing beforehand, so you know what to expect by breaking the problem down into manageable proportions and by figuring out strategies for coping, before the situation itself actually arises.

You can also try adopting the philosophy advocated by Scarlett O'Hara in *Gone with the Wind*. When faced with a seemingly insoluble problem she would say, "I'll think about it tomorrow."

Scarlett was a pretty good psychologist.

12
Stress-A Review.

STRESS, AS WE HAVE SEEN, IS A LARGE, COMPLICATED, AND
sometimes confusing subject. But understanding stress
and learning how to deal with it effectively are extremely
important. In the preceding eleven chapters we have
looked at stress from a number of different angles: what it
is, what the causes of it are, and how best to keep the stress
in your life at a tolerable level.

Now it's time to review the main points that we have
covered.

Understanding Stress

- Stress is the body's general response to *any* demand made upon it.
- Stress is physical. It causes real and measurable changes in many of your bodily functions, such as your blood pressure, your hormone production, your lymphatic system, and more.
- Your body can tolerate certain levels of stress. But excessive stress can make you physically ill. It can also make you emotionally depressed, create mental confusion, and lead to irrational behavior. All of these are perfectly *normal* reactions to excessive stress.
- There are three stages to the stress reaction. First there is a sharp alarm reaction, when the body's resistance drops suddenly and dramatically. As the stress continues, there is a longer stage of resistance, where the body's functions appear to return to near normal. If the stress is long term, then the third stage, the stage of exhaustion, is reached, and the body's resistance drops sharply once again.
- Stress can be produced by physical agents such as an injury, or by mental and emotional agents such as fear and anxiety. In the modern world the emotional agents of stress—stressors—are often the most important.
- While stress is usually associated with negative actions or emotions, it is also produced by positive actions or emotions. Winning a prize can be as stressful as losing one; love can be as stressful as hate.
- The body has a fixed supply of adaptation energy. This is the energy that allows you to adjust to change. Adapta-

tion energy is depleted by stress. During periods of low stress, your supply of adaptation energy available for immediate use is rebuilt by drawing on deeper stores of energy.

Stress and You

- Each of us is unique and each of us responds differently to stress. Some thrive under a load of stress that would cause others to collapse.
- When calculating the amount of stress we are under, it is vital to take into account all of the sources—including bad weather, an infected toe, as well as the horrible fight you have just had with your parents. Even if nothing dramatic has just happened to you, you still may be subjected to a lot of stress.
- Though the problems associated with excessive stress in adults have been given the most attention, excessive stress is not just an adult problem. The teenage years are a time of unprecedented change, both physical and social. Change results in stress, and so despite what you have been told, instead of these being the happiest years of your life, they may be the most stress filled.
- Young people also have an abundant supply of adaptation energy and are able, therefore, to recover from the ill effects of excessive stress more rapidly than older people.

Coping with Stress

- Since small, repeated irritations or little hassles account for much of the stress in our lives, doing something about them can be one of the most effective ways of lowering the total load of stress we face, particularly when we can't solve some of the big problems in our lives.
- Don't underestimate the value of time. The fatigue and depression that so often result from the stress of a major event, such as the breakup of an intense relationship, eventually go away because of the body's natural ability to restore adaptation energy. You don't have to *do* anything. The process is entirely automatic. But it takes time.
- Specific stress can be relieved by switching the stress to another part of the body or mind. For example, if you are feeling tired after studying, getting out and taking a long walk or run—switching the stress from mind to body—might actually make you feel less tired.
- Physical activity, from running to exercises to relaxation techniques, can help to relieve the muscle tension caused by stress and thus reduce the ill effects caused by stress in general.
- Mental stress can often be coped with effectively by "thinking about something else," not worrying about a problem while in a highly stressed state, or by simple meditation which helps to "give the mind a rest."
- Attempting to avoid all stress is neither possible nor wise. The body and mind appear to need an outlet for their energies. If they don't have proper and productive out-

lets, these energies turn destructively inward. Thus boredom, monotony, and isolation can be extremely stressful.

- Trying to reduce the uncomfortable and unpleasant feelings caused by excess stress through the use of drugs or alcohol is counterproductive and can be dangerous. Drugs and alcohol can have a powerful effect on the body—causing stress. Instead of lowering stress, you actually increase it.

- Risk taking is another dangerous and ultimately ineffective method of coping with the negative side of stress. Some risk taking is a necessary part of being young. However, getting "drunk on your own hormones" is just as stressful as getting drunk on alcohol. Therefore, using risks to cope with the stress of boredom or the stress of a bad family situation is merely adding more stress to your life when you don't need any more.

- As Hans Selye has said, "stress is the spice of life." The exhilaration and the depression and the highs and the lows of your stressful teen years are part of life. Enjoy the highs and try not to dwell on the lows.

Stress and the sometimes almost crushing feelings that it may provoke are a natural and inevitable part of life, particularly during your teen years. These are years of change, and there can be no change without a lot of stress. But nature has equipped you superbly to survive the stress and to profit from it. You can come out of stressful times stronger than you ever were before.

Bibliography

Boston Women's Health Collective. *Ourselves and Our Children.* New York: Random House, 1978.

Bottle, Helen. *Parents' Survival Kit: A Reassuring Guide to Living Through Your Child's Teenage Years.* New York: Doubleday Publishing Co., 1979.

Breton, Myron. *How to Survive Your Child's Rebellious Teens.* Philadelphia: J. B. Lippincott Co., 1979.

Bright, Deborah. *Creative Relaxation.* New York: Harcourt Brace Jovanovich, 1979.

Brown, Barbara. *Stress and the Art of Biofeedback.* New York: Harper & Row, Publishers, 1977.

Bruch, Hilde. *The Golden Cage: The Enigma of Anorexia Nervosa.* New York: Random House, 1979.

Eagan, Andrea. *Why Am I So Miserable If These Are the Best Years of My Life?* New York: Avon Books, 1976.

Freudenberger, Herbert, and Richelson, Geraldine. *Burnout: The High Cost of Achievement.* New York: Doubleday Publishing Co., 1980.

Giovacchini, Peter. *The Urge to Die: Why Young People Commit Suicide.* New York: Macmillan Publishing Co., 1981.

Guardo, Carol J., ed. *The Adolescent as Individual.* New York: Harper & Row, Publishers, 1975.

Hendin, Herbert. *Suicide in America.* New York: W. W. Norton & Co., 1982.

Hyde, Margaret O., and Forsyth, Elizabeth. *Suicide: The Hidden Epidemic.* New York: Franklin Watts, 1978.

Klagsbrun, Francine. *Too Young to Die: Youth and Suicide.* Boston: Houghton Mifflin Co., 1976.

Madison, Arnold. *Suicide and Young People.* New York: Clarion Books, 1978.

McCoy, Kathleen. *Coping with Teenage Depression.* New York: New American Library, 1982.

Miller, Mary Susan. *Childstress!: Understanding and Answering Stress Signals of Infants, Children and Teenagers.* New York: Doubleday Publishing Co., 1982.

Noble, Jane, and Noble, William. *How to Live with Other People's Children.* New York: Hawthorn, 1977.

Norman, Jane, and Harris, Myron. *The Private Life of the American Teenager.* New York: Rawson, Wade, 1981.

Rabkin, Brenda. *Growing Up Dead.* New York: Abingdon Press, 1979.

Richards, Arlene, and Willis, Irene. *How to Get It Together When Your Parents Are Falling Apart.* New York: David McKay Co., 1976.

Selye, Hans. *The Stress of Life,* rev. ed. New York: McGraw-Hill Book Co., 1976.

———. *Stress Without Distress.* Philadelphia: J. B. Lippincott Co., 1974.

Spilke, Francine. *What About the Children?: The Divorced Family, a Parent's Manual.* New York: Crown Publishers, 1979.

Walker, Eugene. *Learn to Relax: Thirteen Ways to Reduce Tension.* Englewood Cliffs, N.J.: Prentice-Hall, 1978.

Index